THE TRAGIC LIFE OF LADY JANE GREY

'There is a time to be born and a time to die, and the day of our death is better than the day of our birth'

Lady Jane Grey, written during her incarceration
in The Tower of London

'Good people, I am come hither to die, and by a law I am condemned to the same.'

Lady Jane Grey, The Tower of
London 12th February 1554

THE TRAGIC LIFE OF LADY JANE GREY

Beverley Adams

PEN & SWORD
HISTORY

AN IMPRINT OF PEN & SWORD BOOKS LTD.
YORKSHIRE – PHILADELPHIA

First published in Great Britain in 2024 by
PEN AND SWORD HISTORY
An imprint of
Pen & Sword Books Ltd
Yorkshire – Philadelphia

ISBN 978 1 39905 270 2

A CIP catalogue record for this book is available from the British Library.

Typeset in Times New Roman 12/16 by
SJmagic DESIGN SERVICES, India.
Printed and bound in the UK by CPI Group (UK) Ltd.

Pen & Sword Books Limited incorporates the imprints of Atlas, Archaeology,
Aviation, Discovery, Family History, Fiction, History, Maritime, Military,
Military Classics, Politics, Select, Transport, True Crime, Air World,
Frontline Publishing, Leo Cooper, Remember When, Seaforth Publishing,
The Praetorian Press, Wharncliffe Local History, Wharncliffe Transport,
Wharncliffe True Crime and White Owl.

For a complete list of Pen & Sword titles please contact
PEN & SWORD BOOKS LIMITED
George House, Units 12 & 13, Beevor Street, Off Pontefract Road,
Barnsley, South Yorkshire, S71 1HN, England
E-mail: enquiries@pen-and-sword.co.uk
Website: www.pen-and-sword.co.uk

or

PEN AND SWORD BOOKS
1950 Lawrence Rd, Havertown, PA 19083, USA
E-mail: uspen-and-sword@casematepublishers.com
Website: www.penandswordbooks.com

Contents

Acknowledgements

I am very aware there have been many books written about the tragic life of the 'nine-days queen' Lady Jane Grey, but I felt so connected to her story that I wanted to add my own contribution to that ever-growing list.

Many thanks to all at my publisher Pen & Sword, especially Jonathan Wright for allowing me the opportunity to write this book, thank you for your continuing faith in me. To Laura Hirst for all the hard work and support she has put into all my books to date.

As always, thanks to Mum, Dad, Chris, Paul and Alison. To Mary, Danni and Luke with a special mention to Faith, Kai and Kali. To my wonderful and supportive friends Marie Drelincourt, Lorraine Mawdsley, Kathryn Baxendale, Leona Steele, Chris Smith, Gill Parker, Carol Worster and Pat Palmer with a special mention as always to Emma Powell.

Huge thanks to all the historians who have gone before me for your wonderful works that drew me into wanting to know more about Jane and to all the wonderful archivists for their hardwork.

Finally, thank you to Lady Jane Grey, Queen of England. She was but a sixteen-year-old girl whose life was cut tragically short, a young woman who showed true bravery and who never wavered when faced with the most terrifying of ordeals. Writing her execution was one of the most heart-breaking passages I have ever worked on and breaking through the myths brought forward the rawness of her untimely death. She was inspirational, courageous and brave beyond any words I could ever put down here but I hope I have done her justice.

Timeline of Events

3 March 1515	Mary Tudor, Queen of France marries Charles Brandon, Duke of Suffolk in France against the wishes of Henry VIII
18 February 1516	Birth of Princess Mary at the Palace of Placentia, Greenwich
17 January 1517	Birth of Henry Grey at Westminster, London
16 July 1517	Birth of Frances Brandon at Hatfield, Herts
25 June 1533	Mary, Duchess of Suffolk dies aged 37 at Westhorpe Hall, Suffolk
1533	Frances Brandon marries Henry Grey
1534	First Act of Succession and the Act of Supremacy passed in Parliament
1536/7	Lady Jane Grey is born, probably in London
June 1536	Second Act of Succession is passed in Parliament
12 October 1537	King Edward VI is born at Hampton Court Palace
25 August 1540	Lady Katherine Grey is born at Bradgate Park, Leicestershire
February 1544	Third Act of Succession is passed in Parliament
20 April 1545	Lady Mary Grey is born at Bradgate Park, Leicestershire
28 January 1547	King Henry VIII dies at Whitehall Palace, Westminster
February 1547	Lady Jane Grey becomes the ward of Thomas Seymour
May 1547	Thomas Seymour marries Katherine Parr
June 1548	Jane travels to Seymour's seat at Sudeley Castle

5 September 1548	Katherine Parr dies shortly after giving birth to a daughter
7 September 1548	Lady Jane Grey is Chief Mourner at the funeral of Katherine Parr
September 1548	Jane returns home to Bradgate Park, Leicestershire
October 1548	Jane returns to the household of Thomas Seymour at Seymour Place
17 January 1549	Thomas Seymour is arrested
20 March 1549	Thomas Seymour is executed on Tower Hill, London
11 October 1549	Lord Protector Somerset is arrested
November 1549	Jane visits the Lady Mary at her home Beaulieu
December 1549	The Grey family celebrate Christmas at Tilty
June 1550	Roger Ascham visits Bradgate Park for the first time
11 October 1551	Henry Grey is created Duke of Suffolk
November 1551	Jane is part of the welcoming party for Marie de Guise
22 January 1552	Lord Protector Somerset is executed at Tower Hill, London
25 May 1553	Jane marries Guildford Dudley
June 1553	King Edward VI's 'Devise for the Succession' is signed
6 July 1553	King Edward VI dies, Jane becomes Queen of England
10 July 1553	Jane is openly proclaimed the new queen
19 July 1553	Jane is deposed as queen and Mary Tudor is proclaimed Queen of England
22 August 1553	Duke of Northumberland is executed on Tower Hill, London
5 October 1553	Act of Repeal is passed in Parliament
13 November 1553	Jane and Guildford are tried and found guilty of high treason and are condemned to death at the Guildhall

February 1554	The Wyatt Rebellion is suppressed
12 February 1554	Lady Jane Grey and her husband Guildford Dudley are executed
23 February 1554	Henry Grey, Duke of Suffolk is executed on Tower Hill, London
17 November 1558	Queen Mary I of England dies at St James's Palace, London, her half-sister Elizabeth ascends the throne as Queen Elizabeth I
20 November 1559	Frances Grey, Duchess of Suffolk dies
26 January 1568	Lady Katherine Grey dies at Cockfield Hall, Suffolk
20 April 1578	Lady Mary Grey dies in London

Introduction

On the 8 September 2022 the reigning Queen of England passed away at Balmoral Castle, Scotland after a record breaking seventy years on the throne. The death of Queen Elizabeth II set in motion a centuries old protocol which sees a new monarch succeed to the crown. The death of Queen Elizabeth brought her eldest son to the throne as King Charles III in what was a seamless transition. King Charles was proclaimed king by the Accession Council on the 10 September at St James's Palace, London and proclamations were then read out across the capital cities of the United Kingdom. The Accession of King Charles was assured from the day of his birth, but not every royal accession through history has been as straight forward.

In 1135 upon the death of Henry I his only surviving legitimate child was a daughter called Matilda, she was set to take the throne as per her father's wishes. The nobility had sworn allegiance in front of Henry to support Matilda when the time came but as soon as the old king was dead they switched their support to her cousin Stephen of Blois, an act which put the country on the path to civil war. The very idea of a woman ruling over men was too much for those councillors to bear and they preferred to support a weaker claim if that meant having a male ruler. Another succession crisis loomed in 1714 when Queen Anne died childless and with parliament not willing to accept a catholic monarch of either gender, they looked to their cousins in Hanover, Germany to take the throne. This signalled the end of the Stuart reign in England and would later lead to the Jacobite rebellion of the mid-eighteenth century.

Nowadays the heir to the throne is known before the monarch dies, the rules of primogeniture state it is the right, by law or by custom, for the first-born legitimate child of the monarch to inherit the throne. These rules had been altered from agnatic primogeniture, meaning the eldest son automatically inherits, by the Succession to the Crown Act 2013 when the then Duchess of Cambridge was expecting her first child with her husband Prince William. Queen Elizabeth decreed that child would one day inherit the throne regardless of its sex. Prince George was born on 22 July 2013, however when his sister, Princess Charlotte was born on 2 May 2015 the new rules meant she would outrank any younger brothers she may have so when Prince Louis was born on 23 April 2018 he did not displace his elder sister in the line of succession. The claiming of the throne of the United Kingdom is now done by absolute primogeniture.

The accession of King Charles III was unchallenged but nearly 470 years earlier at the Tower of London a young woman aged just 16 years old was proclaimed queen following the death of her cousin the king, but her accession was far from smooth. The late king, Edward VI, had died childless at the age of just 15 years old meaning the appointment of the next monarch was perhaps not as straight forward as it ought to have been. Edward made the decision to go against the wishes of his father, Henry VIII, and amend the line of succession by appointing his cousins daughter Lady Jane Grey as his successor. By doing this he was overlooking the claims of his popular half-sisters the Ladies Mary and Elizabeth and first cousins Frances (Jane's mother) and Eleanor Brandon. (The Scottish line of Henry VIII's elder sister Margaret Tudor had previously been discounted and Edward was happy for this omission to remain) The accession of Lady Jane Grey was controversial from the start, going against the wishes of Henry was a bold move on Edward's part but what he failed to realise was that the Catholic Mary was popular amongst the people. Henry VIII, who commanded absolute loyalty from his people, clearly stipulated his eldest daughter by the well-loved Queen Katherine of Aragon, should be crowned queen if Edward failed to produce a legitimate heir. But Edward was willing to overlook this and his request set in motion a sequence of events that led Jane to become known as the 'Nine Days Queen'.

When approaching the writing of a book about a person as well-known as Jane you must leave all your preconceptions at the door if you are going to write a narrative that is true to your own findings. Most of us know the story of the nine days queen, or at least we think we do. We know that we are taught in our school history books about the young girl forced to take the crown to please power-hungry men, but is this portrayal true or is there more to Lady Jane Grey than meets the eye? Was she more than just a pawn to the ambitious men that surrounded her? Was she ambitious herself, she may not have sought the crown but once it was hers was she reluctant to let it go? Perhaps she coveted the crown of England from the start and relished the thought of being queen. In this book I don't claim to have unearthed some long-lost piece of evidence that turns this tragic story on its head, rather it is a look a Jane herself, the person she was, how her fate moulded her into the protestant martyr we know so much about today. It looks at her childhood and the relationship she had with her family and it considers how much pressure they applied to her and what affect her upbringing had on the fateful events of 1553/4.

Looking back over nearly 500 years is not easy, not every conversation and detail was recorded and blanks need to be filled and we fill them as best we can, based on the evidence available to us. At first glance the evidence suggests that Jane was a meek and mild young woman who was brainwashed by her parents to accept a throne that was not hers for the taking. But further investigation shows us a Lady Jane Grey who comes across as a strong-willed and stubborn young woman who was not afraid of upsetting those around her. She was firm in her religious beliefs and held no prisoners when it came to religious debate making her a well-respected theologian across Europe. The question that fascinated me the most was what our perception of Jane is now and do we consider her to be a true queen of England or was she just a usurper in an attempt to keep England protestant? There are many facets of Lady Jane Grey's short life and here I attempt to tell her tragic story.

Chapter 1

Tudor Origins

As dawn broke over the Tower of London on 12 February 1554 a young girl aged just 16 years old prepared to die. In just a few short hours she would be made to walk through the blood of her dead husband and step onto the scaffold, a structure she had watched being built from her prison window, a structure which would soon become her place of execution. As a convicted traitor she was to be beheaded by the orders of her cousin Queen Mary Tudor.

How did Lady Jane Grey, the great niece of Henry VIII and former queen of England, come to find herself in such a precarious position? There have been many theories put forward that suggest she was nothing more than a mouthpiece for her power-hungry father-in-law the Duke of Northumberland which is probably a fair assumption to make, but having Tudor blood coursing through her veins was probably the biggest reason she found herself facing the axeman on that bright but cold February morning. Whether the blame did lay at the feet of Northumberland or even with her parents was irrelevant, in the end she was a threat to the stability and safety of Mary's throne and because of that she had to die. It is heart-breaking to see a girl on the cusp of womanhood so cruelly used by the men who rather than exploiting her should have been there to protect her from harm, to make sure she was safeguarded from ever having to face her own execution. In fact, the only man who did remain with Jane at the end was her husband Guildford and he sadly shared her fate.

There is no getting away from the fact that Jane was an important young woman because she was a member of the royal family and that made her a very lucrative catch in the marriage market. You may have expected her father, the Duke of Suffolk to have made a noble and worthy match for his eldest child. One that would bring the family wealth and status, a sensible match rather than a hare-brained scheme. Unfortunately for Jane, he was not a sensible man, or rather, he was not a man with much sense and one who was easily led. Sadly, all this would become apparent, much to his daughter's despair.

We know that Jane's life ended on the scaffold, but what about her early life and childhood? In order to understand the person Jane was and the position she held within the Tudor royal family we must go back and look at her ancestry. Her father came from very noble stock, he was Henry Grey, 3rd Marquess of Dorset, later the Duke of Suffolk and the Greys were a well-respected family. Henry was a great-grandson of Elizabeth Woodville, the wife and queen of King Edward IV, by her first husband Sir John Grey of Groby. But Jane's royal blood came through her mother Lady Frances Brandon. She was the eldest daughter of Charles Brandon, Duke of Suffolk and Mary Tudor, dowager Queen of France and the youngest and favourite sister of King Henry VIII. This made Frances a granddaughter of King Henry VII and Elizabeth of York, who incidentally was the eldest child of Edward IV and Elizabeth Woodville making her and Henry distant cousins.

Princess Mary Tudor was born on 18 March 1496 at Sheen Palace, London, she was the youngest surviving child of King Henry VII and his queen, Elizabeth of York. In 1514, at the age of 18 years old the beauty of the English court sacrificed her future and freedom when she agreed to marry the ageing King of France at her brother, the king's request. It was nothing but a dynastic match and it was hoped the marriage would build better relations between the two countries. Cardinal Wolsey had brokered a peace treaty and part of the deal was that Mary would travel to France and become it's queen. The great scholar Erasmus commented that 'nature never formed anything more beautiful than Mary' she had been described as elegant with a fair complexion and even from early childhood she was considered a true beauty.

The princess crossed the channel with her English ladies and married King Louis XII on 9 October at Abbeville in northern France. When Louis's second wife, Anne of Brittany died on 9 January 1514 from a kidney related illness, he wasted no time in finding her replacement. As with most kings, Louis was desperate for a legitimate son to pass his crown to but despite being married twice before he had not managed to produce the all-important male heir. Unlike England, France was ruled under salic law which meant his two daughters by Anne were unable to claim the throne, despite there being no direct male claimant.

The Anglo-French marriage was not a love match, at least not on Mary's behalf anyway, but it has been described as being mutually friendly and affectionate and the couple often enjoyed each other's company. It has been suggested that Mary and Louis came to an understanding with each other regarding the expectations of their marriage, she was there to sire a son. Sadly, less than three months after the wedding King Louis died from gout, although the rumours at the time suggested his death came about as a result of over exertions in the bedchamber! Even though she did not truly love the king, his death left Mary sad and alone as a widow in a foreign country but as its queen she was obliged to enter a period of forty days mourning. This was a strict period where the young queen lived as a recluse, the purpose of it was to establish if she was pregnant and when it was established she was not she was sent to the Hotel de Cluny in Paris for a further six weeks of mourning. The only male she was allowed to have contact with was the new king, Francois I, who had come to the throne as Louis's first cousin once removed, he also happened to be his son-in-law. It was rumoured Francois wished to marry Mary as his wife Queen Claude was sickly, sadly she was to die in July 1524 aged just 24 years old.

Francois may have had plans of his own for Mary but prior to agreeing to the marriage with Louis she had discussed with her brother her feelings for Charles Brandon, Duke of Suffolk who also happened to be a very close friend of the kings. She declared her love for Brandon and told her brother she would agree to the French marriage on the basis that when Louis died she was free to marry wherever she wished. Henry agreed to his sisters demands and the French marriage went ahead. When Louis died and Mary was confined in her mourning she began to panic that her brother would disregard their agreement and marry her off again for political gain, there was talk of a Spanish match. In her panic, Mary wrote to Henry pleading to remind him of his promise:

> Sir, I beseech your grace that you will keep all the promises that you have promised me when I took my leave of you by the waterside. Sir, your grace knoweth well that I did marry for your pleasure at this time and now I trust you will suffer me to marry as me liketh for to do. . . wherefore I beseech your grace for to be a good lord and brother unto me.

It is unclear as to what Henry's true plans were for his sister at this stage but given that she had written reminding him of his promise and knowing of her love for Suffolk it seems slightly strange that he would send Brandon to escort his sister back to England. Was he testing their loyalty? He must have had absolute trust in his friend not only to bring his sister home safely but to only deal with Mary and her practical affairs and nothing else. Henry requested Suffolk swear an oath that he would not to marry his sister whilst they were abroad. Given her young age Henry would still be looking to use Mary to forge a foreign alliance and could not afford for her to marry at her own behest, regardless of what promises he had made to her, she was still a valuable commodity for England.

The thought of another political marriage horrified her so much it left her in floods of tears, she pleaded with Suffolk to marry her whilst they had the chance to do so as she was convinced the second she set foot on English soil Henry would have her tied up to someone else. It was not an easy choice for Suffolk, he owed everything to Henry, they had been close friends since boyhood and he held a genuine affection for him, they were almost like brothers. In the end they defied the king's wishes and the clandestine marriage took place in 1515 at Hotel de Cluny, in Paris with just a handful of guests present, including King Francois who no doubt revelled in scuppering his great rivals plans. In Mary's eyes she had made the sacrifice her brother had asked of her for the good of the country and should have been allowed to marry as she wished as he had promised

The challenge now facing the newlyweds was how to break the news to Henry. Suffolk wrote to Thomas Wolsey and confessed what they had done and asked him to tell Henry on their behalf. When Henry found out he was outraged; he could not believe that his closest friend would betray him in such a way, especially after he had given his express orders not to the very thing he had gone and done! Once the feeling of anger had subsided Henry felt hurt and betrayed by their actions and if they thought they were going to get away with a slapped wrist and a telling off they were sadly mistaken. Henry was angry and that put Charles in grave danger, he was not overly popular due to his closeness to the king and the last thing the council would have wanted was him gaining more power over them. All they could do was throw themselves on Henry's mercy and hope he would be willing to forgive them which he did after a while but it soon became apparent that his forgiveness would come at a hefty price. He banished them from court and fined them £24,000 (approximately £13 million today), they would also have to stump up the cost of Mary's first dowry and every other cost involved in her French wedding, she would also have to hand over all the jewels she had gained from the French marriage. Charles knew he was taking a huge risk in marrying the princess but luckily for him Mary was Henry's favourite sister and the couple got off relatively lightly all things considered. Mary was protected by her royal status but Charles, a man from humble beginnings in Suffolk, had committed high treason by marrying a royal princess without the consent of the monarch and the punishment for treason was execution. Princess Mary was lucky to have her royal status to protect her but as their granddaughter would learn nearly forty years later it is not always a foregone conclusion that having royal blood would save you from the axe.

It was certainly a hefty price to pay but thanks to Wolsey's intervention Henry's displeasure would not last long and the couple finally arrived back in England in May. On 13 May they held a grand wedding ceremony at Greenwich which the king attended, it looked like they had finally been forgiven. The fine was so heavy they could not afford to reside at court very often, Charles would visit in his capacity of Duke of Suffolk and as a member of the council whilst Mary remained behind at their country residence of Westhorpe Hall in Suffolk. Her banishment from court came at a convenient time as she also had an intense dislike of Anne Boleyn and often refused to attend court because of this. The former Queen of France did not agree with the treatment of her friend, Katherine of Aragon, at the hands of her brother and this would be a point of discontent between the two siblings which came to a head when Henry married Anne in 1533.

The marriage of Charles Brandon and Mary Tudor caused a huge scandal at the English court. Many were concerned it would give him even more power and influence over the king now he was his brother-in-law, but Charles was likeable and had shown his worth as a soldier and courtier, and with Mary being so well loved it meant the marriage was accepted amongst the courtiers. Between them they became a Tudor power couple, it would seem all was forgiven and the couple settled into married life.

Charles Brandon was the son of Sir William Brandon and Elizabeth Bruyn. Sir William was Henry VII's standard bearer at the battle of Bosworth and was cut down and killed by Richard III. As a result of this and for the loyalty served, Henry VII took in Charles as his ward which meant he was brought up at court and soon became close friends with Prince Henry. As the two lads grew into young men, people often mistook them for brothers as they were tall, and athletically built. Brandon rose high through the ranks and Henry VIII created him Duke of Suffolk on 4 March 1514 following his performance during the French campaign of 1513. By the time he married Mary he had already been married twice before, firstly to Margaret Neville which was later dissolved, and then to marry Anne Browne with whom he had two daughters, Anne passed away in 1511. Following the death of Anne, Brandon was contracted to marry Elizabeth Grey, 5th Baroness Lisle, it was from her he took the title Viscount Lisle but when the contract was annulled he surrendered the title.

It appears the Brandon marriage was a true romance and looks to have been happy. The couple had four children together, a son called Henry was born in March 1516, Frances the eldest daughter was born in July 1517 followed by her younger sister, Eleanor in 1519 and another brother also called Henry in 1523 which would indicate the elder Henry had died sometime before 1523. It was not unusual in those times to name a younger sibling after the death of the elder one. The younger Henry was created the 1st Earl of Lincoln on 18 June 1525 at the age of 2 years old by his uncle the king. Brandon had wanted to arrange a marriage between Henry and Catherine Willoughby, a young heiress in her own right, sadly Henry would die in childhood and Brandon would marry Catherine himself following the death of Mary thereby keeping her vast lands and wealth in Brandon hands.

Lady Frances Brandon was born at Hatfield, Herts, the seat of the Bishop of Ely, in 1517. The name Frances was very rare at this time and it has been suggested Mary chose it to honour her French connections, Frances being the female form of Francis/Francois. Children were often named after family and friends and appears the naming of Frances was nod to King Francois I of France for his assistance in helping the two lovers marry. If this is true one can only imagine how Henry VIII felt about having his niece named after his great rival. Frances was christened at the nearby church, her god-mothers were Queen Katherine of Aragon and her 5-month-old daughter Princess Mary who had been named after her aunt.

The Brandon children spent much of their childhood at the family seat of Westhorpe Hall in Suffolk, they had plenty of space to play and run around in and were often joined by their cousins Princess

Mary and the Lady Margaret Douglas, the only daughter of the elder Tudor sister Margaret and her second husband Archibald Douglas, Earl of Angus. Mary was a loving aunt and made her home a safe and welcoming refuge for Mary and Margaret who had both suffered from their bickering parents' marriage fall outs. They were also joined by Anne and Mary Brandon, Suffolks elder daughters from his earlier marriage. The childhood of the Suffolk children was a care free time, no doubt the duchess protected them as much as she could from the machinations of court, especially during the time of the King's 'Great Matter' when Katherine of Aragon was being displaced for the sake of Anne Boleyn.

As the nieces and nephew of the king of England the Brandon children held a high place in the line of succession, Henry only had one daughter, the Princess Mary, and it looked unlikely he would have any more children with his wife, Katherine of Aragon. Given that the kings elder sister Margaret's children were of Scottish descent and the law at the time stipulated that any claimant to the throne had to be born on English soil, the Brandon children were sitting fairly high up the order of succession. The young Earl of Lincoln was a very real candidate to be King of England should Henry sire no male heir. Even though England was not ruled by salic law, which meant a daughter could inherit if she had no brothers, it was no sure thing Mary would inherit her father's throne if she had a male cousin.

But times changed fast at the Tudor court and soon enough the King would divorce Katherine and marry Anne Boleyn in the hope she would give birth to the eagerly anticipated son. Unfortunately for Anne she did not provide the king with his male heir, like Katherine before her she only gave Henry a girl, Elizabeth. Anne paid the ultimate price for not giving Henry what he wanted when she was executed on trumped up charges of adultery, incest and treason. Anne's death cleared the way for Henry to marry Jane Seymour and she gave birth to the future king Edward VI in 1537. Sadly, the young Earl of Lincoln died at the age of around 11 but during his short life he had the two most important attributes that a royal heir needed, he was male and he was English born. His death meant Prince Edward was the sole male heir in the line of succession, it was a precarious position and one that caused Henry VIII much concern.

Charles Brandon was well-known as being a man who was always looking to strengthen his dynastic hopes when an opportunity arose. He did this through his marriages and through the marriages of his children. In 1535 he arranged for his younger daughter Eleanor to marry Henry Clifford, the future Earl of Cumberland. The Cliffords held vast swathes of land and power across northern England, including castles in Skipton and Brougham. It was considered a very good match for Eleanor but for her elder sister Frances, he chose Henry Grey, 3rd Marquess of Dorset. They were just 16 years old when they married at Suffolk Place in 1533, Henry was six months older than his bride to be and on paper this was a powerful match.

Henry Grey was from a respected family but did not enjoy the same royal lineage Frances did, despite his boasts of royalty. He descends from the Greys of Groby, who can proudly trace their line back to the time of William the Conqueror but it was not until the fifteenth century when the family had a taste of royal life. His great-grandmother Elizabeth Woodville married King Edward IV and it was then the family really come into prominence. Before her marriage to Edward, Elizabeth had been married to Sir John Grey, a Lancastrian knight who fought and died at the Battle of St Albans in 1461, that marriage produced two sons, Thomas and Richard. Thomas would become the 1st Marquess of Dorset and the grandfather of Henry; Richard would be executed by King Richard III in 1483. Thomas Grey married Cecily Bonville and amongst their many children was another Thomas, 2nd Marquess of Dorset whose second marriage to Margaret Wotton produced six children including Henry, the eldest son. Henry and Frances were both the great-grandchildren of Elizabeth Woodville so you can see where Henry got his ideas of royal grandeur from but he had no royal blood in his veins.

Henry Grey was born on 17 January 1517 at his father's estate Bradgate Park in Leicestershire. At the time of his birth, Henry's father, Thomas, was in high favour with Henry VIII, for who he was named after. The loyalty meant the young Henry enjoyed time in the household of the king's illegitimate son Henry Fitzroy, Duke of Richmond and Somerset. Thomas would carry the sword in the ceremony that saw Fitzroy have his dukedoms conferred on him. The two boys became firm friends during the time they spent together and it seems to have been a happy household especially when they were joined by other lads their ages including William Parr, the younger brother of Katherine Parr, later queen of England. Henry enjoyed his studies, amongst the subjects he would have learnt were Latin, French and the classics. He was clever and engaged well with his tutors, a trait his daughter Jane would later inherit. He appears to have been popular and easy to get along with but for all his knowledge and intelligence, he lacked application and any real common sense, something that would let him down on many occasions, with fatal consequences.

On 10 October 1530 Thomas Grey died meaning Henry became the 3rd Marquess of Dorset at the age of just 13. His father had been one of the wealthiest men in the country at the time of his death due to his vast estates. He held land in sixteen counties in England including over 100 manors meaning his death made Henry a very rich and eligible young man. Despite his new found wealth and the urge to splurge, his mother realised education was still important and a provision had been made to pay his tutor £20 a year (£8,825). Thankfully Henry could see the importance of being well educated and willingly agreed to carry on with his studies. As a minor he was unable to gain full access to his inheritance until he turned 21 years of age. Until he reached his majority, his mother Margaret Wotton would control the purse strings, much the Henry's annoyance. Margaret Wotton was Thomas Grey's second wife and he her second husband. She was well connected and would stand as god-mother to the princess Elizabeth in 1533 but her good standing was tarnished over her treatment towards Henry when in 1534 she was deemed to be an 'unnatural mother' over the lack of generosity she showed towards her son. His peers felt she was treating a nobleman with close links to the king in an inappropriate manner. It is a fair assumption to make that Henry and his mother did not always see eye to eye, their relationship was often strained and like most teenagers who feel hard done by, Henry rebelled. The details are scant but whatever he did resulted in him being banished from court for two months as punishment and from that time onwards a close eye was kept on him to keep him inline. Despite the close relationship his father had shared with Henry, the king would never fully embrace him in the way he did his father.

As he grew older, Henry began to indulge in the vices of other noble men including hunting and gambling and before long his debts began to spiral out of control but with no male figurehead to guide him it was difficult to see how he was going to rein in his excesses. He was later described as 'young, lusty, and poor, of great possessions, but which are not in his hands, many friends of great power, with little or no experience, well learned and a great wit'. His behaviour was starting to ring alarm bells at home so his mother wrote to Thomas Cromwell requesting that she be allowed to visit her wayward son at court in an effort to keep him in check. In a bid to bring Henry to heel and as an opportunity for Margaret to pass over the worry of her son to someone else, Charles Brandon bought his wardship in March 1533. As mentioned before, Brandon was always on the lookout for a way to strengthen his ties and he made no exception here. He knew that by buying Henry's wardship meant he would one day be able to negotiate his marriage, and with two daughters needing husbands it was a very shrewd move on his part.

He may not have been cash ready but at the age of 21 Henry was set to inherit a vast fortune, including land and property making him a good catch for any noble lady looking for a husband. Unfortunately for Brandon, there was another noble young lady who had already been betrothed to Henry, Katherine Fitzalan, the daughter of the 11th Earl of Arundel had been promised in an agreement that saw Henry's sister Katherine marry Henry Fitzalan, Arundel's son. This posed a huge problem for the duke, for as he well knew, a betrothal in Tudor times, regardless of the age of the bride and groom, was a legally binding agreement. Therefore, Henry and Katherine were as good as married and releasing him from this would cause a scandal at court. It would also cost a small fortune as compensation would have to be paid to the unfortunate brides family, this is not to mention the humiliation Katherine would have to endure as a jilted bride.

Once Henry got wind of a potential plan to marry him to Frances he point blank refused to marry Katherine; Frances was a much better catch, she had royal blood and brought many more advantages than Katherine ever could, he is clearly marking out his ambition at an early age. It is not clear when the break came but letters from his mother would indicate she was not happy at the amount the family would have to pay to free Henry from his obligation but seeing that at this time Henry was the ward of the king it is likely he intervened to smooth out the situation. Also, the breaking of a marriage contract like this would be frowned upon at court and presumably pressure was applied to the youngster to force the marriage, these letters are dated November 1532 which would also indicate Suffolk was arranging his wardship as early as then but needed this cleared up before he committed.

Once the betrothal had been broken and the compensation settled nothing could stop the marriage between Frances and Henry from going ahead. As was normal practice amongst the nobility, multiple marriages were arranged at the same time so Eleanor's betrothal to Henry Clifford was also negotiated at the same time.

The marriage contract between Henry and Frances was agreed on 24 August 1533 but the marriage did not take place at once as there were things to be agreed upon before it could. Once again, Henry's mother had her say and wanted assurances from Suffolk that he would support the couple financially and remove that burden from her. He agreed to her terms and offered to support the couple until Henry reached his majority at 21 when his inheritance shall be his own. It was also around this time the duchess of Suffolk began to show signs of illness, she had never really recovered from her bout of sweating sickness she caught in 1528 and sadly she died at Westhorpe Hall on 25 June 1533 at the age of 37. Her cause of death is unknown and many theories have been suggested but with a weakened constitution she could have succumbed to almost any illness.

Her death was recorded by Charles Wriothesley, an officer of arms at the College of Arms in the following extract:

> This yeare, on Midsommer eaven, died the French Queene, sister to the Kinge, and wife to the Duke of Suffolke, and was buried at Saint Edmondsburie in Suffolk'

Following her death, her body lay in state at Westhorpe for three weeks before being moved for burial. Frances was the chief mourner and in recognition to their former queen, the French sent a delegation to England to attend the funeral on 22 July when she was interred into the crypt at Bury St Edmunds Abbey. Her coffin was pulled by six horses and in the procession came 100 torch bearers, members of the clergy and nobility, including Suffolk's yeomen. A full requiem mass was heard and just prior to her interment there was a scuffle when her step-daughters pushed their way to the front of the cortege, no doubt much to the upset their half-siblings. When her brother Henry VIII dissolved the monasteries just five years later, Mary's remains were moved to St Mary's Church, Bury St Edmunds. Her remains were caused even further unrest when in 1784 they were disturbed once more when her coffin was opened by Horace Walpole and Dorothy Bentinck, Duchess of Portland. They took locks of her hair before sealing the coffin back up, since that point Mary Tudor, Dowager Queen of France and Duchess of Suffolk as laid at rest. Her death caused much grief, she was well liked and well loved by the people and no doubt her passing caused great grief for the king.

There are no exact records of the wedding ceremony between Henry and Frances, even the date is not clear but it must have happened sometime after the marriage contract was agreed and before the beginning of February 1534. Given her status as niece to the king it was no doubt a costly affair with the bride and groom decked out in sumptuous attire. We do know it took place at Suffolk Place, the mansion and London home of her father and it is more than likely the king and queen were in attendance given the close family links and Suffolks friendship with the king. Make no mistake though, this was a marriage brokered by the duke of Suffolk for political gains and certainly not for love, love in Tudor marriages was a happy by-product, you married to improve your family's connections. A woman of Frances's station would have known from a young age that she would be married as per her father's wishes, her mother would have prepared her and Eleanor for a life as a wife to a wealthy powerful man. The unification of the great houses of Suffolk and Dorset was the overall aim, if the young couple happened to fall in love, then that was merely a bonus. Thankfully, it appears the young couple got on from the start and it turned out to be a good match. Frances was one of the most important ladies of the land, she often took precedence after the king's daughters, out-ranking the Lady Margaret Douglas who came from the superior line and even though Margaret was born on English soil her mother's line was considered inferior due to its Scottish connections. But despite her elevated status she would have to wait until her husband turned 21 to take the title of Marchioness of Dorset as the current marchioness, Henry's mother, was alive and using the title. Margaret Wotton would attain the title of dowager marchioness when Henry reached his majority and Frances would step into her shoes.

Frances would have received some level of education in how to run a large household, her mother would have ensured she was well-equipped to perform her role as wife to a noble man with vast estates. But as her mother had passed away, in order to prepare her for this role Frances entered her mother-in-law's household. It was not unusual for a young lady to enter the household of another great lady to learn the ropes, she may have looked to enter the household of her new step-mother but given she was only 14-years-old that was not really a feasible option. Suffolk wasted no time in re-marrying when just three months following the death of his duchess, he married Katherine

Willoughby. Willoughby was the daughter and only surviving child of Maria de Salinas, one of Katherine of Aragon's Spanish ladies-in-waiting, and the wealthy landowner William Willoughby, 11th Baron Willoughby de Eresby. When the baron died her wardship fell to the king and he then sold it on to Suffolk on 1 March 1528. At the time of the marriage Suffolk was 49 years old but Katherine was a very wealthy young lady, she was originally betrothed to the Earl of Lincoln but given their young ages the marriage never happened and the ever-ambitious Suffolk, keen to keep hold her fortune and lands, decided to marry her himself. Despite the large age difference Katherine would go on to bear him two sons who would tragically die just an hour apart from sweating sickness in 1551 aged 15 and 13. Frances had a good relationship with her step-mother, after all they were only two years apart in age and would have spent time together at Westhorpe when they were growing up. Katherine Willoughby was known for being stern and an ardent reformer as well as being one of the country's leading ladies. When she was older she grew close to Bess of Hardwick and the Lady Margaret Douglas, Countess of Lennox and even helped facilitate a marriage between Bess's daughter Elizabeth Cavendish and Margaret's son Charles Stuart, much to Elizabeth I's disgust. She would later marry for love and have children with a member of her household named Richard Bertie.

Not long after the marriage ceremony, Henry returned to court and Frances went to her mother-in-law, presumably at Dorset House on the Strand. Henry's relationship with his mother had always been strained and how she felt about taking Frances under her wing we do not know but at least if she trained her daughter-in-law then there may be some hope the Dorset estates would be well maintained and looked after. Henry and Frances seem to have got on well from the start, they seem to have been pleased with each other, it was clearly a political marriage but Suffolk experienced no arguments from Frances when he suggested Dorset as a husband and her mother seems to have been content with the choice too, sadly she did not live long enough to see either of her daughters marry. The initial separation must have left them both frustrated but they were young and understood they had plenty of time to get to know each other better. Frances was well known throughout her life as being punchy and formidable and Henry seems to have been content to let his new wife make the major decisions that came up. She was clearly the dominant partner which just showed up how weak-willed her husband was, a trait that would plague him throughout his life and cause him to make decisions that would tear his family apart. He needed Frances to be the decision maker as he had no skill for it, she was the one guiding the couple through the dangerous maze of the Tudor court, she was after all a fiery red head with Tudor blood in her veins, it has even been suggested that in later life she began to resemble her uncle Henry in terms of her expanding waistline and tyrannical behaviour.

And so, the couple settled into married life. It is believed Frances gave birth to a baby boy who died in infancy although there are no official records to confirm this but she was soon pregnant again and in 1536/7 gave birth, this time to a girl they called Jane.

Chapter 2

From London to Bradgate

Details surrounding Jane's birth are scant, we do know she was born sometime in late 1536 or early 1537 either in London at the family's palatial home of Dorset House on the Strand or as tradition dictates at their country seat at Bradgate Park in Leicestershire. Many modern historians believe her date of birth to have been in the latter part of 1536. Despite the fairytale romance of Jane being born at a manor house in the English countryside, it is unlikely to have been at Bradgate given that the family did not officially take up residence there until 1538. Prior to that it was the home of Henry's mother Margaret Wotton, it is not impossible that Jane was born here, but unlikely. Jane's ambiguous start to life was not unusual, records were not always accurately kept in the sixteenth century, especially for the birth of an inconsequential girl, even if she was of royal blood. The birth of a girl was often overlooked and celebrated without much pomp.

Giving birth at this time was a perilous activity and every care was taken to ensure the safety of the mother and a safe delivery of the child, both physically and spiritually. Being a woman of high rank, Frances would have no doubt followed the customary rules for a royal birth which had been laid down by her great-grandmother Lady Margaret Beaufort in her manual *Ordinances for a Royal Birth* (see Appendix One). The manual was written to offer guidance to Margaret's daughter-in-law Elizabeth of York as she prepared to give birth to her first child, Prince Arthur. Despite it being written specifically for Elizabeth it became the go-to handbook on how a royal birth ought to be conducted. The duchess of Suffolk would have no doubt followed the same process when she gave birth to Frances and in turn Frances would more than likely have followed the same rules.

Prior to the birth a chamber would have been selected and made ready following the rules of the handbook. Frances would then have entered into confinement at approximately four to six weeks prior to her expected due date. Saying goodbye to her husband and household she would have given herself over into the care of a group of carefully selected women, usually family members or those of rank who had already given birth. The plan was to make the birthing chamber as hot and dark as they could, regardless of the time of year, so a fire would be lit in the hearth and the windows and doors sealed shut. The only light would come from the fire and candles which were placed around the room. The purpose of these measures was to protect the mother and baby from any evil spirits that could enter the chamber and cause harm. Rich embroidered tapestries adorned the walls and they would have been of a biblical nature and contained nothing that could frighten the newborn as it entered the world. This made for a stuffy and oppressive atmosphere, it must have been overwhelming for a first-time mother like Frances and she would not have had her mother on hand to reassure her, she had to put her life and that of her unborn child in the hands of these women and hope all went well.

Of course, childbirth at this time was strictly an all-female affair and the birthing chamber a female only domain, no man was to cross the threshold until after the baby had been delivered, including the father. The couple would have attended mass together to pray for a safe delivery, he would then have walked his wife to the birthing chamber and bid her farewell at the door which would then be sealed shut, he would not see her again until she had given birth. Being a loving husband Henry would no doubt have stayed close by awaiting news of the delivery. But just like the sex of the baby nothing was guaranteed. Childbirth was dangerous, the mother was vulnerable and open to infection, there were no hygiene rules to follow and no antibiotics available should things go wrong. Many women died either during childbirth or from the after effects of it with many haemorrhaging or contracting a fatal infection like puerperal fever. Even having the best midwives and physicians available can prove useless, Queen Jane Seymour was an example that no woman was completely safe after she died giving birth to the future Edward VI. The birth was especially difficult and she laboured for two full days and three nights before finally giving birth to the kings long awaited son and heir. Soon after Prince Edward's christening it became apparent to all the queen was not well and she died twelve days later. Frances's grandmother Elizabeth of York died shortly after the birth of her daughter in 1503, no woman was safe, not even a queen.

As far as we are aware Frances came through Jane's birth with no issues, there is speculation she may have had two previous pregnancies in which she gave birth to two boys but there is no evidence to support this, but if she had, then she had already experienced the heartbreak of losing a newborn, or having a stillbirth. If this is true she must have entered the birthing chamber with a sense of dread, would it happen again, or worse still, would she succumb to the childbed? Whilst the news of a pregnancy was a happy occasion and the birth of a child a cause for celebration, there was always a sense of dread and fear, for the mother and the father. In the end, the only disappointment Frances may have felt was that she had given Henry a daughter rather than the much-desired son. Henry would have met his baby daughter for the first time once she had been cleaned, swaddled and settled in the royal nursery. Giving birth to a son and heir was the main role of a woman of rank in Tudor times and Katherine of Aragon and Anne Boleyn both suffered for their supposed failure in only giving birth to girls, but there was nothing to suggest that Henry and Frances were disappointed with their new arrival, he was probably just relieved his wife had survived for surely sons would follow. They were both young and Frances had proved she could carry a child to term and give birth with no issues.

As soon as she was born, baby Jane, named after her great-aunt Queen Jane Seymour, would have been placed into the care of a special team of handpicked nurses. As was the custom for the day, Frances would not have been expected to be involved in any of the practical duties and would have had very little to do with the day-to-day care of her daughter. This was not down to any attachment issues but being a noble woman meant Frances's duties lay elsewhere, like seeing to her husband's needs, running her household and attending to court life. Despite not having the constant care of her mother Jane would still have had the very best care, Frances would have chosen the nursery household very carefully, they may have been recommended by other women and would have been well vetted. Jane was a very important little girl and her rank and status demanded the very best of carers. The team would take care of every aspect of Jane's care and would have included maids, servants, a wet-nurse to feed her until she was ready to be weaned and rockers to rock the infant in a specially made cradle to help soothe her to sleep. Once the nursery household had been established Frances would have taken a step back and left them to care for her child, only to be called upon should there have been any urgent need, for example if Jane had fallen ill. If Frances was in residence with her daughter she would more than likely have visited the nursery daily to check on her daughter's progress and to reassure herself that all was running well.

Jane's baptism would more than likely have taken place shortly after her birth, this was not unusual given the high mortality rate amongst infants and it was important the baby was prepared to be received in heaven should the worst happen. Queen Jane was listed as her godmother but sadly there are no other details remaining of the ceremony. We could speculate that Eleanor or the Lady Mary may have stood as the other godmother and may be even the king stood as godfather to his niece's first born. Frances's return to court was only possible after she had gone through the churching ceremony in which she would have been purified by the priest, this usually took place approximately six weeks after the birth. Once she had been churched, Frances could return to court life and more importantly to her husband's bed and her baby would begin her life in her sumptuous nursery.

The year 1536 turned out to be an eventful one for the Tudor family, the queen, Anne Boleyn was executed at the Tower of London on 19 May following her spectacular fall from grace, she left behind her daughter Elizabeth who was aged just 2 years old. Not only did the young Elizabeth lose her mother but she also lost her title and place in the line of succession. She was no longer to be known as Princess Elizabeth but instead suffered the same fate as her elder half-sister Mary and was demoted to the rank of Lady and declared illegitimate. With his two failed marriages and two illegitimate daughters Henry VIII instigated the Second Act of Succession. The first Act had been ratified in 1533 and it declared the then Princess Elizabeth his heir presumptive, the place that had previously been held by the Lady Mary, this was a decision that caused upset at court as not many liked Anne Boleyn, including Frances, and loved the old queen, Katherine. But by 1536 he had declared his youngest daughter a bastard and removed both her and Mary from the line of succession completely. This meant the king had no legitimate heir to his throne however, the act did give Henry the provision to name any heir he wished which he declined to do at this time.

A realm without a named heir is a dangerous place, the uncertainty and instability it could cause could lead to civil unrest but there were strong rumours circulating at court that the king was about to name his illegitimate son Henry Fitzroy, Duke of Richmond & Somerset as his heir. He had acknowledged Henry since his birth and even held celebratory feasts when he was born, he was the living proof he could sire a male child, the embodiment of Henry's manliness. Sadly, Henry Grey's former childhood friend would pass away at St James's Palace in July 1536 aged just 17 years old. Earlier that year the king married Jane Seymour and with that came fresh hope for a legitimate male heir. To great joy Queen Jane would give birth to the future Edward VI in 1537 and the issue seemed to be resolved. After a wait of nearly thirty years and following a break with Rome and the catholic church Henry VIII finally had his legitimate male heir, he finally had his prince.

The king had moved heaven and earth to get this child, he broke the country away from Rome, divorced one wife and executed another so when the little prince made his arrival he made sure everyone knew.

He ordered the canons to be fired at the Tower of London, bonfires to be lit in the streets and the church bells to toll. Unlike Jane, whose arrival was celebrated quietly amongst her family, her second-cousin Prince Edward was given a lavish christening at Hampton Court, his eldest half-sister, the Lady Mary stood as his godmother alongside the Duke of Norfolk and Archbishop Cranmer who stood as godfathers. The four year old Lady Elizabeth carried the chrism, she in turn was carried by Edward's uncle Edward Seymour, Earl of Hertford. Following the baptism, Prince Edward was confirmed and Charles Brandon, Duke of Suffolk stood as his sponsor. The fact Mary and Elizabeth were included in the ceremony is a good indicator as to what the king's relationship was with them at this time. Sadly, Henry's joy was not to last when just two weeks after the birth of her son, Queen Jane died. Both Henry and Frances had prominent roles at her state funeral.

The death of queen Jane devastated the king and left the infant prince Edward motherless. So much expectation was placed on Edward and any childhood illness, fall, bump or bruise caused great anxiety for king Henry. All the king needed to do was keep Edward safe and reign long enough until his son reached his majority age so he could rule alone. The court was once again getting twitchy, all their hopes of a peaceful accession were thrown into chaos with just one male heir and the queen dead, things were on a knife edge. A child was a fragile thing in Tudor London and history did not bode well for kings who were minors when they inherited their thrones. In 1377 Richard II was just 10 years old when his grandfather Edward III died passing the throne to his grandson. Richard struggled to reign successfully and was deposed in favour of his Lancastrian cousin Henry Bolingbroke, the future Henry IV. Richard was imprisoned in Pontefract Castle where it is believed he was starved to death. Henry VI suffered a similar fate. He inherited the throne at just 9 months old in 1422 and his fractured reign was littered with war, instability and mental illness. He was eventually murdered in the Tower of London supposedly on the orders of Edward IV, Henry VIII's grandfather. The most famous child-king was Edward V, he was aged just 12 years old when he disappeared along with his younger brother Richard, Duke of York in the Tower of London. They were declared illegitimate and their uncle Richard III claimed the throne in place of Edward in 1483, they became forever known as The Princes in the Tower. Their deaths have been subject to much debate which continues to this day. All this evidence would indicate that kings who inherit their thrones young tend to have a tricky time of things. So, when Edward gained his crown in January 1547 the country held its breath.

With just Prince Edward as his heir and with the king now unlikely to have any further children, Henry, now in his early fifties, decided to amend the succession yet again. A later Third Act dated 1543 would restore the Tudor sisters to the line of succession but critically it did not restore their legitimacy. They took their place behind Edward and any children he may have, but by leaving his daughters status as illegitimate Henry left them open to scrutiny and vulnerable to threats. He may have thought it would never be an issue as Edward would one day marry and have children of his own but as he well knew having a legitimate son was not always an easy task. Mary and Elizabeth were now unprotected and should the crown come to them they would be open to challenges. If Edward failed to have any legitimate children the crown was to go to any children Henry may have had by his then wife Katherine Parr or any future wife he may have but given his age and ill health this was highly unlikely.

In 1538 Henry Grey turned 21 meaning he could finally take legal control of his wealth and estates. It also signified he was free from any further interference from his mother and he and Frances were now financially independent and no longer needed to be reliant on her father to support them. But with this new found wealth came the responsibility of running their own households, Frances's training could finally be put to use. It also meant they could finally make the move north from London to the family seat at Bradgate Park in Leicestershire. Bradgate Park sat in the Charnwood Forest approximately five miles to the north west of Leicester. It was an expensive new build home which replaced an existing building on the site. It had been the seat of the Grey family since its completion in around 1520 and was built by Henry's father, the 2nd Marquess of Dorset. The house sat in acres of stunning peaceful parkland; it was built of red brick with lighter coloured brick cornerstones. Upon arrival, visitors would be greeted by a large gatehouse which at either side stood large towers complete with ornamental chimneys. The house was two stories high and had been constructed around a 'U' shaped courtyard. The west wing housed the family's private rooms, it also housed a bakery, brewery and had its own servants quarters allowing the family to enjoy a retinue of live-in servants to tend their needs all day, every day. The windows were large, a sign of wealth as glass was very expensive, they also allowed plenty of natural light to flood the 80-ft long great hall which would have been the centre of the house. There was also a chapel for the family's use and which no doubt became a place of refuge for Jane as she grew older. It was here that Jane and her family lived for much of her childhood, sadly, not much remains of the house but you can still get a sense of its Tudor grandeur and some say Jane's ghost haunts the ruins at night. The Greys were definitely royalty in the Midlands, holding court in their magnificent home where Jane would be raised to fully understand her royal lineage.

Bradgate had been the home of Henry's mother since the death of her husband so it is understandable why she felt such a connection to the building but Henry had never enjoyed a warm relationship with his mother and his request for her to move out caused further friction between the pair. Margaret Wotton even went as far as writing to Thomas Cromwell pleading her case, she stated that her son had not even let her take her personal belongings with her, she also claimed she was in poor health, but Henry was within his rights to evict his mother from his property. The treatment of his mother casts Henry in a very bad light as he comes across as a heartless and callous son but did he make these decisions himself? This leads us to question how much influence Frances exerted over her weak husband to finally get her own country home. Margaret Wotton died in 1541 and at the time of her death the relationship with her eldest son was still fractured, although perhaps in a slightly better state than it was in 1538. The young Grey family hastened to Leicestershire to take up residence, finally Frances had her own home, her own finances and a title. As Marchioness of Dorset, she held sway over many, she was royal, she was titled and now the mistress of a grand estate, after years of marriage the couple could now finally settle into family life.

According to tradition it was at Bradgate Park on 25 August 1540 that the couple's second child was safely delivered, a daughter named Katherine. Apparently named for Queen Katherine Howard who had married the king just a month before her birth. Katherine joined her elder sister Jane in the nursery. Five years later another daughter was born on 20 April 1545, Mary completed the nursery and no more children would be born to Frances and Henry. There are lengthy gaps between the births of each daughter which may indicate there had been other pregnancies and possibly other children born that died either during or shortly after birth but no records exist to confirm this. Whether the couple were disappointed by the lack of a son is not documented but given how important it was for a nobleman to have an heir it surely must have been somewhat disheartening and whether Frances carried with her a sense of failure again we do not know. What we do know though is that the couple had three healthy daughters and they were to be brought up understanding their importance in the world and each one was going to leave her own tragic mark on it.

It was here nestled deep in the Leicestershire countryside the young Lady Jane Grey would spend most of her childhood. Cosseted away from court at her parent's country home where she had ample space to play and romp around the vast gardens and forest with her younger sisters. Unbeknownst to them what the future held, the sisters were ignorant of what lay ahead and how in just a few years' time their family would be decimated. They were to become entangled in numerous plots, some of which were of their own making and some of which were not.

Chapter 3

Early Childhood at Bradgate

As the Grey sisters grew older they were taught to respect their royal lineage and also the House of Grey. Over time each girl developed her own character and personality becoming her own person. Katherine, the middle sister, was considered to be the most beautiful of the three siblings. She is described as having long golden hair and bright blue eyes, a typical English rose if you will and with her good looks came a bubbly and friendly personality. She was fun and adventurous with a love of animals, plays and masques. Jane could not have been more different to Katherine, she is said to have been serious and devoted to her studies, happier indoors reading a book than outside in nature or at play. In terms of her looks, Jane was described as having brown eyes with the signature Tudor auburn hair like her mother. She was quite short in height but was graceful with a slim figure, some would say pretty, if not perhaps a beauty. Her temperament is described as being fiery, a classic Tudor trait, she also developed a stubborn streak as she got older and began to know her own mind from a fairly young age. Unfortunately, unlike Katherine and Mary, we have no definitive portrait of Jane, there are many that claim to be of her but in reality we cannot be 100% certain, it is possible her portraits were either destroyed or hidden away following her death.

The age gap between Jane and Mary of ten years meant the youngest sister tended to look towards Katherine when it came to bonding and having someone to play with but it was obvious from a very young age that Mary was suffering from a deformity of the spine which gave her the appearance of having a hunched back. As a consequence of this Mary appeared small for her age and was often ridiculed and taunted at court. The Spanish ambassador cruelly remarked she was 'little, crooked-back and very ugly' but much to Frances and Henry's credit they did not closet their daughter away as many noble families would have. To have a child born with any kind of deformity was seen as a sign from God that he was displeased, it was even seen as a mark of evil but the Greys were not ashamed of their youngest daughter and treated her in the same manner as they did Jane and Katherine. But sadly, for Mary she was not considered a beauty like Katherine, and neither did she have the same level of intelligence that Jane had, but she was kind and had a warmth to her that made her affectionate. She never really outshone either sister and struggled to find her place in the world of Tudor royal court life but it is more likely that history does not remember her because she did not cause as much controversy as her sisters, that is not to say she was completely free from scandal, she, like her sisters incurred the royal wrath of fury. Katherine on the other hand would make her mark on the royal court for all the wrong reasons and like Jane, incur the displeasure of another Tudor cousin. More on that later.

As members of the royal family the children would have followed strict daily regimes, probably very similar to that of their mother and grandmother before them. They would have been taught to defer to their parents in all things, but as granddaughters to a queen, they too were to be respected. A typical day would begin at around 7am for prayers, the sisters were brought up as evangelicals, just like Prince Edward, and despite Frances and Henry being born and raised catholic, they too had embraced the new religion that had swept the country. Henry was seen as one of the country's leading reformists, he was a religious fanatic with connections that stretched right across Europe, something he would later pass on to his eldest daughter. Following prayers at around 8am the sisters would break their fast with a small meal of meat, bread and ale, the main meal of the day would normally start between 10am and 11am and could potentially last a few hours given the number of courses available and depending if guests were visiting Bradgate. The food would be brought at the same time giving the family an opportunity to sample whatever dishes they wished. It would be a rich diet containing meat and Bradgate Park had a bountiful number of deer to choose from. There would be fish courses and pastries all made using herbs and spices and covered in thick rich sauces. The savoury courses would be followed by a sweet course, washed down with ale or wine. Following the meal, the children would go to their studies for the afternoon, stopping for a light supper about 5pm. They would retire to bed about 8pm, if they were at home with their parents then they would visit them before bed to be given their blessing, the girls would say their prayers before clambering into their luxurious beds. It appears the days were relatively easy, no doubt some recreational time would be worked into the schedule for those that wished to get outside to ride or play. They led a privileged life as the great nieces of Henry VIII and cousins to Edward VI.

The description above is of an average day but Frances and Henry were popular in the local area and tended to socialise when they were home from London, they would bring with them the latest news and gossip from court that no doubt their neighbours lapped up. The Grey family had been based in the area since around 1490 when Henry's grandfather, the 1st Marquess of Dorset, began to build a new family home. From that time, they had been the highest-ranking noble family in the county and when Henry married Frances that brought royal glamour to the area. Often relatives would be invited to Bradgate to dine with the family especially Henry's brothers Thomas and John which gave the sisters an opportunity to get to know their uncles well. They were more than likely closer to their Grey relatives than their Tudor ones given the short amount of time they spent in London in their early childhood. There was no reason for the Dorset's to be in residence at court given their father held no office under Henry VIII. Considering they were royal children they grew up in relative obscurity in the midlands and this anonymity would later be an issue for Jane during her short-lived role as queen.

But for the time being the Grey family were happily ensconced in the Leicestershire countryside where they could enjoy the hunting which was excellent at the well-stocked Bradgate Park, it made for an idyllic childhood, with the enormous grounds to play in. Bradgate Park offered the Grey sisters the chance to grow up surrounded by nature. They would walk their father's greyhounds, go deer hunting and it is even said Henry had a tame bear that no doubt thrilled the children. It was a world away from the court in London, Bradgate afforded Jane and her sisters a childhood that Prince Edward could only have dreamed of having. Henry and Frances were a very sociable couple and liked to gamble and attend social functions in Leicester, having children did not hinder their ability to enjoy a good social life. But the flip side of living the high life meant the finances took a hit and neither Frances nor Henry were good with money and soon enough they were racking up debts. Whilst their parents were off entertaining or being entertained, the girls were left in the capable hands of the household staff, it was not the duty of noble parents to raise their children, they had a whole household for that but a distant relationship could lead to tensions as the children grew older, especially for Jane.

Being children with royal blood the Grey sisters had certain expectations placed upon them from birth. Their behaviour had to be exemplary at all times and whilst having high aspirations for them Frances and Henry did not spoil or over indulge their daughters. That was considered to be an unflattering trait, spoiling children made them feeble and weak, that said, they had toys as any normal child would have had but given their elevated status they were remarkably restrained. The Dorsets did however place a high value on education and they decided that all three of their daughters were to be educated to the highest possible standard. Many noble families of the time felt the education of girls was not necessary but there were some that bucked this trend. Sir Thomas More for example placed high value on the education of girls, his eldest daughter Margaret Roper became a translator and writer and was considered to be the most learned woman in Tudor England she was in fact, the first non-royal woman to publish a translated work. Erasmus praised her for her work and she proved women could and should be educated as they were just as capable of academic work as men. Sadly, Margaret was the exception, not the rule as the young girls and women of most families were only trained in practical subjects that would enable them to run a household effectively and very few were educated in academic subjects.

The very highest of women were often well educated and this was one of the main reasons for ensuring Jane, Katherine and Mary were fully educated. When the inevitable comparisons came between them and their Tudor cousins they could be compared favourably alongside the ladies Mary and Elizabeth who as the daughters of a king had been educated well. We know that Henry Grey received a very good education and he was known, even on the continent, for his intelligence especially when it came to theology. We can only assume Frances received a good standard of education given the rank and status of her parents although there is no records that comment on this.

Like all children of their rank, from an early age the girls would have been taught how to behave well, most importantly they would have been instructed on how to have impeccable manners and be obedient to their elders. They would only speak when spoken to, they were to never place themselves in a conversation when they had not been invited to do so as that was seen as being presumptuous and forward. If they were asked any questions they would be expected to answer politely, promptly and clearly and only answer that question alone, they were never to proffer their own opinion if they had not been asked to give it. Their table manners would have been perfection, they must eat cleanly, politely, they must never guzzle their food and would have been taught to use utensils delicately. As young ladies they would have been complemented on their behaviour and would graciously take any praise they were given. They must never be argumentative or rude and under no circumstances were you to show yourself up, you were a representation of your family and if you misbehaved then the good name of your family was at risk.

Sadly, these were not rules Jane, or her sisters come to that, would always follow.

Whilst academic education was a luxury for some there were subjects that all noble girls were taught. The main role of a daughter in an aristocratic family was to marry well, your father, or highest male relative should your father be unable to, would arrange your marriage as would best suit the family. In other words, a marriage that would bring good connections and wealth and as the daughter it was your responsibility to make sure you were ready to undertake the role of housewife and mother when the time came. Many men wanted a wife who was obedient to them and girls were brought up to accept they were inferior to men, to all men, and that was the case within a marriage. It did not matter if you were a queen or a peasant, the role of a woman was the same, you were expected to keep a good home for your husband and provide him with a son and heir. If you were a woman of noble birth then you would be expected to marry a man of the nobility and many of those had large country estates that she would be expected to run smoothly.

In order to accomplish this, girls would have been taught how to sew, embroider and keep accounts. They would also be taught the basics of cooking so they would be able to have an opinion on the best dishes to serve at a banquet. Knowing how to hold such an event would be critical and at Bradgate Frances would have been heavily involved in the arrangements of any entertainment they wished to host. At these banquets the women would be expected to sing and dance and maybe even play a musical instrument to entertain the guests. These were skills a young women could show off and any young girl who had aspirations to go to Court had to have these accomplishments if she was looking to attract a husband.

As Jane was the eldest of Frances and Henry's children more effort was put into her formal education than the two younger girls. Katherine and Mary would have been expected to marry well but Jane was the star prize in the marriage market and her parents had to make sure she was prepared. But even though much attention was given over to Jane, Katherine and Mary also received an excellent standard of education. The girls education was heavily influenced by their father's reformist beliefs and Jane's formal education would have started around the age of 5. From an early age she showed promise of following her father's aptitude for learning. She was clearly an intelligent child who enjoyed her studies and would have begun her education by learning her letters and numbers and reciting the Lord's Prayer. Once she had mastered that she would have progressed onto reading books and learning subjects including history and languages including French and Latin. When she was a bit older she also learned Greek which turned out to be a revelation for her as it led to her love of reading the Greek philosophers and translating many texts. Whilst Jane excelled at the more academic side of learning she also had to learn the more feminine skills such as needlework, dancing and music which were all desirable skills in a young lady of her rank. There was no getting out of that but we do not know how Jane took to these lessons as the focus has always been on her intellectual prowess.

Jane as always comes across as being a girl that loved to learn, one who absorbed knowledge and who was always keen to study. Unfortunately, her younger sisters did not share the same enthusiasm and thirst for knowledge but they too would have been expected to reach a certain level of knowledge but they just weren't bookish kind of girls. Katherine would have enjoyed the singing and dancing and Mary often followed her lead but there was still a requirement for them to be trained in the practical subjects.

The marquess and marchioness of Dorset would have taken time and great care over choosing the right tutors for their daughters. The man in charge of teaching Jane was John Aylmer a Norfolk born scholar and later Bishop of London. He had been sent to Cambridge to study by Henry Grey after spotting his early potential for learning. Once he had left Cambridge Henry offered him a place in the household at Bradgate as his chaplain and tutor to the sisters. He was instructed to teach Jane Greek which she soon found a love for, she was an ideal pupil as she never ceased to want to learn and was always looking for her next subject. Tuscan Michelangelo Florio was tasked with teaching Jane Italian and Latin and as a devout Protestant he was also appointed her chaplain. Florio was an ardent supporter of Jane and when her failed bid to become queen ended he fled England for the safety of Protestant Switzerland.

Aylmer was to become one of the most influential people in Jane's life, they held a strong sense of respect and admiration for each other and under his guidance she thrived, much to her parents delight. He advised Jane to follow the example of Lady Elizabeth and not to be frivolous with her dress, it was best if she wore only plain clothes. He also advised her to ignore Lady Mary, a piece of advice she would later regret. Aylmer, like Jane would never come to terms with people who held differing religious beliefs to them, both were zealots and had very little time for those who failed to agree with them. Because of this attitude many wanted Aylmer removed from his position of Bishop of London, he was considered a much better scholar than he was a Bishop. Aylmer was the driving force behind Jane's thirst for religious education, like her father, who no doubt encouraged his daughter's religious enthusiasm. They put Jane on a path that played a part in her eventual downfall, her inability to reason with others was not considered a pleasant trait.

As Jane grew older her desire for knowledge grew with her. Her books were her safe place, she found solace amongst the Greek philosophers, she could understand their reasoning and often delved into the pages of her beloved tomes to escape. Despite having two younger sisters to play and engage with Jane's childhood was lonely, she had no real friends to speak of and she does not appear to have formed any close bonds with other girls her age. Her books were her friends and she invested endless hours to learning and devoted her time to her religion. Like Aylmer and her father, Jane had a strong desire for religious reform that bordered on fanatical.

Chapter 4

Religious Upheaval

At the end of 1546 it was clear to everyone that Henry VIII was ill and unlikely to live much longer. His servants and those close to him were too frightened to admit this as predicting the death of a king was classed as treason. But Henry knew, he did not need his physician to tell him his time was coming so he decided to make amendments to the succession and so on 30 December he altered his will one last time. The king may have thought the future of the Tudor dynasty was secure with Edward and any sons he may have, but Henry knew better than anyone how fragile life could be. He saw his elder brother, Prince Arthur die aged just 15, leaving him the sole male heir of his father Henry VII. As Prince of Wales Arthur had been sent to live at Ludlow Castle where he trained to be king. His death came as a devastating shock to his parents who now only had one male heir. Henry's mother, Elizabeth of York would die in childbirth in an attempt to provide the much needed 'spare' for her husband. Henry VIII battled hard to have one legitimate male heir, he had no luxury of the spare heir, all his hopes lay on the young Prince Edward. But Henry had to be pragmatic in his approach in ensuring the Tudor line continued so he named the illegitimate Mary and Elizabeth to follow their half-brother should no legitimate heirs of his body be born. Interestingly it was at this point Henry decided to discount the line of his elder sister Margaret completely from the succession. Margaret had been married to the Scottish King James IV with whom she had one surviving son, King James V, who was ruling at the time Henry amended his will so it is understandable he would not want him to amalgamate England into Scotland. But Margaret then went on to have a daughter by her second husband, the Earl of

Angus and that daughter was Margaret Douglas, later the Countess of Lennox and she had been born in England and brought up at Henry's court. The king had a good relationship with his niece, forgiving her indiscretions and arranging her marriage to Matthew Stewart, Earl of Lennox, he even placed Margaret on the same social standing as his daughters. Margaret was close to Lady Mary and spent much of her youth with Frances and her younger sister at Westhorpe. It is understandable why Henry wanted to discount a Scottish claim, at that point any claimant to the English throne had to have been born within the realm, clearly James V wasn't but Margaret Douglas was which makes her omission from the succession interesting, perhaps the thought of Matthew Lennox becoming king worried him and with him being Scottish made the king's mind up.

If we take this into account we can understand the omission of Margaret Tudor and her descendants but we do not know the logic behind the omission of Frances and her sister Eleanor, they were supplanted in the line by their daughters. So, Jane would follow Elizabeth then would come Katherine and Mary with finally Margaret Clifford, Eleanor's only child. We can perhaps apply the same logic as with Margaret Douglas, Henry clearly did not relish their husbands taking the throne alongside their wives and effectively ruling as King. This is understandable with Frances and Henry, we know the king did not value him as he never placed him in an office of power and despite Henry Grey being intelligent and likeable and the husband of his niece the idea of him as king must have worried Henry greatly. But the same cannot be said for Eleanor's husband, she married Henry Clifford, 2nd Earl of Cumberland in 1535 and he had been a true and loyal servant to Henry, successfully defending the northern borders against the Scots so that same rule cannot apply to him making the omission of Eleanor questionable. Perhaps because he decided to overlook Eleanor, he could not look to place the younger sister in a position of power just because he did not value the husband of the elder one. Therefore, if one was to be discounted, then both must be which is the thinking of Edward when he decided to overlook his half-sisters. It was easy to discount Mary because of her religion so by removing her it became easier to remove Elizabeth. The other option could be that as they were both still of childbearing age then it was feasible they could have a son that would have supplanted them anyway, but is that not also true of all the other women in the line? Any one of them could have a son and heir so why were the Brandon sisters treated in this manner? Maybe Henry still held a deep-rooted resentment for their parents marrying without his permission. Regardless of the reason, for which we will never know, the line of succession at the time of Henry VIII's death was as follows:

1. Prince Edward
2. Lady Mary
3. Lady Elizabeth
4. Lady Jane Grey
5. Lady Katherine Grey
6. Lady Mary Grey
7. Lady Margaret Clifford

In the end the will was irrelevant as none of Henry's offspring had children of their own and as Elizabeth decided against marrying when she was queen she knowingly brought the Tudor dynasty to an end and England looked north to Scotland and King James VI, who became King James I of England in 1603. For all Henry's determination to see the Tudor dynasty carry on for generations, the Scots and Margaret Douglas ruled in the end for James, was her grandson through the marriage of her eldest son, Lord Darnley and Mary, Queen of Scots. It is through her bloodline that the royal family still thrive today.

On 28 January 1547 King Henry VIII died at the Palace of Whitehall leaving his nine-year-old son Edward to assume the throne as King Edward VI. Given his young age, Henry realised Edward could not rule alone so he appointed sixteen executors to form a regency council to help him rule until he reached his majority at the age of eighteen. A member of that council was Edward Seymour,

1st Earl of Hertford and uncle to the young king, he was appointed, or should we say, he self-appointed himself as Lord Protector so he could rule solely over Edward. To bolster his new position, he quickly created himself the Duke of Somerset and his brother Thomas was created Baron Seymour of Sudeley and the Lord High Admiral, which Somerset did to appease his younger brother who felt he should have had an equal share of the power. The news was not so good for Henry Grey, Marquess of Dorset, for he was not one of the original sixteen, despite being one of the country's highest-ranking nobles. Also, given Frances's close proximity to the throne this was a huge snub for the Greys and confirms that Henry VIII did not favour Dorset at all. But to be fair to Henry VIII Dorset had never shown any aptitude for politics, he never showed any willing or want for power so the king was never going to entrust his precious son's early reign to him. It was clear that people thought Henry Grey was ineffectual, lazy and inept.

With Somerset now the da facto ruler of the country he needed allies and as a committed reformer and with his daughter sitting third in line for the throne, Henry Grey quickly became a person of interest. His first prominent role was at the coronation of Edward VI which was held on 20 February 1547 at Westminster Abbey. In the May he was finally admitted to the Most Noble Order of the Garter, a chivalric order that was founded in 1348 by King Edward III. The number of members is strictly limited to twenty-four and membership can only be bestowed by the monarch, Henry Grey, Marquess of Dorset had finally made it. However, Somerset was looking to make a marriage between his eldest son Edward, Earl of Hertford to Jane, Henry declined and quickly saw himself fall out of favour yet again.

With the accession of Edward, England was about to embark on yet more religious upheaval, the new king and the majority of his council were ardent reformists and they were determined to make wholesale changes to the country's faith, much to the delight to the Grey family, this was their opportunity to ingratiate themselves with the young king. During the reign of Henry VIII, it had become dangerous to openly express your reformist leanings but with Edward Seymour assuming power in lieu of Edward VI a religious reform was about to the sweep the nation and the Grey family were at the very centre of it at Bradgate, a well-known hot bed of religious reform. The changes that Edward VI was to make were to be radical, sweeping and utterly transformative to the English church. Catholicism was out and Protestantism was in and if you did not adopt the reformist ways then life was going to get very uncomfortable for you. His changes were praised amongst his supporters, Cranmer hailed him the second Josiah after the biblical king and many saw him as the righteous leader of religious reform and reformists in England. He praised Edward for leading them back to God through his word. Edward expected each one of his subjects to abide by his new rules regardless of who you were and if your didn't then you would be punished as the Lady Mary would find out. He should have realised that his sister was a woman of dogged determination and one that stood by her beliefs and who would even be willing to sacrifice her life for them. She bravely held out against Edward and his men, they tried to bully and cajole her into abandoning the catholic faith but just as she had remained steadfast against her father when it came to acknowledging Anne Boleyn as queen, she remained just as determined against her younger half-brother.

It is not entirely clear if Edward was born a protestant or not, during the reign of Henry VIII being a reformer was still a dangerous thing. When Henry VIII broke with Rome he needed to decide on what basis his Church of England would be based. In 1536 the clergy, nobles and the king came together to decide on ten articles that would help become a compromise between the old religion of Catholicism and the new religion of Protestantism. Despite having the ten articles there was still much confusion surrounding what rules the clergy should be following. A delegation from Europe arrived in London to discuss the situation and they suggested a new set of reforms but Henry was not willing to agree with some of their supposed practices, the delegation left and England remained in religious turmoil. The king wanted religious uniformity in his realm so when a new parliament sat in 1539 he called together the clergy and they came up with six articles, both sides went away to discuss the proposed new articles, there were still some disagreements but finally the Act of Six Articles 1539 was reached. But still there was unrest and Bishop Latimer opposed the act and was forced to give up his diocese as punishment. It is likely Edward embraced the new religion once he became king when he was under the influence of people like Seymour and Cranmer. The reformist faction must have seen an opportunity to spread the reformist word around court, little did they know the young king would take up their cause so enthusiastically. Edward would take notes during the sermons given by archbishop Thomas Cranmer and bishop Hugh Latimer, the latter would become the king's personal chaplain and both would later be executed for their beliefs under Queen Mary. Under their guidance Edward became an evangelical zealot, rather like his cousin Jane, Dorset became much more radical in his religious beliefs during Edwards reign which had an impact on Jane too and both would cross paths with the Lady Mary over matters of religion.

In 1547 the Act of Six Articles was repealed by the Treason Act 1547 which in effect abolished the need to follow the six articles. In an attempt to bring the siblings closer together Edward met with his sisters Mary and Elizabeth at Christmas time 1550. The meeting started lovingly with Edward professing his love for his sisters but things soon turned cold. During Mary's stay a heated and tense meeting took place in front of the court where the king demanded his sister obey him in all things, including her religion. She was reduced to tears; it was a huge embarrassment for Mary and caused such an upset that Edward too began to cry. The siblings were as stubborn as each other and Mary refused point blank to give up the mass she still heard in all her residences, despite it being illegal to do so. Mary even went as far as declaring she would die for her religion if she had to, the last thing Edward, or the reformists wanted was the catholic blood of Mary on their hands. They tried ardently to get her to cede to Edward's way, they threatened her and her staff but she would not relent, they had to accept Mary was an exception to the rules but they would certainly make her life as difficult as possible.

Regardless of when Edward came to the full protestant religion the changes implemented in his name were rapid and caught people off guard which resulted in civil unrest. Not having learnt from the religious uprising in the north in 1536 known as the Pilgrimage of Grace, Somerset allowed religious discord to run rife. In 1548 rebellion broke out in the south west and by 1549 it had spread across southern England to East Anglia, the changes had been too much too soon. All of a sudden with Edward's reign came massive religious upheaval, things had sat very tentatively during Henry's reign but that stability had been shattered. Gone were the religious icons, the paintings on the church walls and much of the liturgy had been removed or amended.

But, the biggest change of all was the introduction of the *Book of Common Prayer* which was first printed in 1549. It listed, for the first time in English, the morning and evening prayer, the Litany and Holy Communion as well as full services for Baptism, Marriage etc.. The book was forced on the clergy and people and its being in English was not widely accepted. At this time all across England various areas spoke their own dialect, there was not necessarily one universal English language, therefore it alienated many of the inhabitants in the south west, in particular those in Cornwall. It was this alienation from the word of God that caused widespread unrest. Edward was adamant the people followed his rule, he was the king and his word was law so he sent royal officers up and down the country to ensure the new rules were being followed as he had ordered. The *Book of Common Prayer* would later be replaced in 1552 when a more revised version would be issued, the later edition had been edited by Archbishop Cranmer and the Act of Uniformity 1552 was passed which authorised its widespread use across the country from 1 November of that year.

Chapter 5

Life with Thomas Seymour

Now aged ten years old, Jane was at an age when her future needed to be discussed. Her marriage was lucrative to her parents, as cousin to the king, Jane was probably the most eligible bride after the ladies Mary and Elizabeth. But, with the tag of illegitimacy staining their reputation and with Jane's prominent place in the line of succession her future husband would have to be from very good stock for there was much at stake, therefore, why not aim for the very top of the pile and marry a king.

Thomas Seymour was a shrewd man on the lookout for power and when he saw an opportunity he exploited it. He saw that Jane was an important young woman so he approached the Greys with an offer that would prove too good for them to turn down. Seymour's audacious plan was to marry Jane to Edward VI thereby guaranteeing her the crown of England as its queen. Seymour knew he had to play this one carefully so he sent one of his men to visit Frances and Henry at Dorset House on the Strand. Sir John Harington was sent to Dorset House to suggest that Jane come and reside with Seymour on the promise that he would arrange a marriage with the king. Harington described Jane as 'a handsom a Lady as eny in England, and that she might be Wife to eny Prince in Christendom, and that, if the King's Majestie, when he came to Age, wold mary within the Realme'. His proposal was that Jane would leave her family home to go and live in Seymour's household. He promised she would complete her education and have access to her parents should she need them. It was not unusual for children of wealthy families to go and live in another household of a similar rank. During their time there they would learn the necessary skills needed for them to take on the future roles expected of them.

For example, young ladies would go into the service of another to learn about household management, if your family was wealthy then you could have found yourself in the household of a great lady which in turn could lead to an advantageous position at court. For young men, they would learn swordsmanship and politics preparing them for a life at court, hopefully in the service of the king.

Unsurprisingly Frances and Henry initially declined Seymour's offer, they felt that he had no authority to be offering such terms when it was his brother that held the power. His access to Edward was limited so how could he expect to negotiate a marriage for him, especially a marriage that Somerset would have to agree to first. And there in lay a problem because the Lord Protector had ideas of his own for Jane. He viewed her as a potential suitor for his own son, Lord Hertford, (who would later go on to marry Katherine Grey) so it was highly unlikely he was going to agree to this match. The Greys and Thomas Seymour saw Edward and Jane as the king and queen of a new England, a reformist England that they would help build and establish as a world leader on the religious stage. Tensions between the Seymour brothers were getting fraught, Thomas felt, as the king's uncle, he too should have some level of power when it came to ruling the country. Edward declined his brothers pleas but when Thomas married Henry VIII's widow, Katherine Parr, he assumed a new level of power, was this a tactical move on his part or did he actually love the former queen? One would like to think the latter was true but Katherine was a respected woman and brought Thomas a new kind of gravitas amongst the Privy Council. The wedding took place far too quickly after the death of King Henry for it to have gone unnoticed and it caused quite a stir but Katherine had always been fond of Henry's children and she had been the only mother Edward had ever really known, the king was more than happy to grant his permission for the marriage between Katherine and his favourite uncle to go ahead. Marrying Katherine was a coup and maybe she would be the key to getting access to his nephew but maybe I am being cynical for there was talk of a love affair before she married Henry VIII, a match that she had no option but to accept.

Thomas Seymour was not to be deterred, he could see the potential of having Jane under his influence and returned with a better offer. If marriage to the king was not enough to tempt Frances and Henry then a payment of £2000 (approximately £550,000 today) would certainly help tip the balance in his favour. He was right, it did the trick and they agreed to send their eldest daughter to live in his household. I find it surprising they were willing to let Jane go for any amount let alone for just £2000. Thomas did not have the leverage to be able to negotiate the king's marriage, that was a matter for the Lord Protector but seeing as he had other plans maybe they felt it was their best option. Being a member of the royal family, the king would have to have given his authority for any marriage that Jane entered so they were technically not free to marry her where they wished anyway. It is hard not to think that even at this young age she is being used for the advancement of others, she was blissfully unaware that she was being moved like a pawn on a chessboard. The other reason for them selling Jane was that their money problems were too great to pass up the prospect of ready cash and their money troubles were no secret. Frances may not have been completely happy with the agreement; she had no great liking for Seymour and Jane was her eldest child, they may not have been close if we are to believe later reports but she would still have had motherly concerns over her child's welfare. But at the end of the day, she had an obligation to back her husband so Jane was passed over into the care of Thomas Seymour.

Jane left the family home in February 1547, leaving behind her parents and sisters she moved to Seymour Place on the Strand. How she felt about the move is not recorded but as long as she had her books and access to education one can imagine she was content and excited for the adventure that lay ahead. Of course, she would not have been told the real reason behind the move, marriage to the king was certainly not discussed with Jane, as far as she was concerned it was a move to aid her advancement and that was all she needed to know. Keeping her in the dark about her future would be a trait people would inflict on her time and time again. It is hard to understand how so many lies and misdemeanours were allowed to have happened to one young girl. How can Jane have been so consistently used for the benefit of others? Safeguarding was obviously something that did not take place in Tudor times but at the very least her parents should have intervened way before it got to a critical stage. The first step of sending her to Seymour was a long path to ruin for poor Jane, and she was totally unaware of the machinations going on behind the scenes. Regardless of what lay ahead, Jane's life carried on as before, Aylmer was allowed to accompany her to Seymour Place and continued to tutor her which no doubt brought her great comfort, she was never happier than when she was with him and her books. The move would have given her a greater sense of freedom and if we are to believe the allegations surrounding her parents and their treatment of her she would have no doubt been relieved to enter a lighter and happier household and that was about to get even happier with the arrival of Katherine Parr.

Knowing she was going into the household of Katherine Parr delighted Jane, and no doubt eased any lingering fears Frances may have had. She was thrilled to be joining the former queen at her private residence in Chelsea where she would also be joined by her cousin, the Lady Elizabeth. Katherine Parr would prove to be a stabling and encouraging influence on the two Tudor cousins and Jane thrived under her guidance. Katherine was of the reformist religion and had previously had printed a religious work titled *Psalms or Prayers taken out of Holy Scriptures* which was published in 1544, in 1545 a second publication was printed entitled *Prayers and Meditations*. Katherine was a deeply religious person and her reformist views nearly found her on the executioners scaffold. She came under increased scrutiny in the early-1540s for being a protestant and things even went as far as a warrant for her arrest being drawn up. Thankfully she was told in advance of the warrant being actioned and she was able to get to her husband the king before they got to her. She managed to placate Henry and the warrant was not spoken of again. Her third publication, *Lamentation of a Sinner* was published in 1547. Katherine was an ideal mentor for Jane and she encouraged her young charge to continue her studies and to be vocal about her religious choices. It was probably around this time, and with Katherine's support, that Jane began to form the religious beliefs that would stay with her for the rest of her life. It was those hardened beliefs that ultimately turned Jane into someone who had no regard for other people's thoughts or beliefs if they did not match with her own then she was not interested in conversing with them and that would be her downfall.

By the age of 11 years old Jane was thriving, much to the delight of her parents, it looked like they had made the right decision regarding their eldest daughter and her future. Despite sharing the same household as Elizabeth there is no actual evidence to suggest what kind of the relationship the cousins shared. They were relatively close in age at just four years apart, both were intelligent and both were reformists so on paper you would think they would have got on and shared a close relationship but that does not seem to have been the case. Elizabeth's tutor Roger Ascham stated that Jane was far more advanced than Elizabeth in educational terms and knowing what we do of her tendency to jealousy it is not hard to imagine there was some level of resentment, especially on Elizabeth's part. The household dynamic was a strange one to say the least because as it stood Jane was Elizabeth's heir. Yet neither girl could ever have imagined they would both one day sit on the throne of England as it's queen regnant, one becoming one of the greatest queens the country has ever known and the other one of the most infamous.

But that summer Elizabeth would have more to worry about than just her clever cousin as Katherine would banish her from her home when she received reports of inappropriate behaviour between her young ward and her husband. Reports tell us Thomas would enter Elizabeth's bedchamber early in the morning and chase the young girl around the room whilst both were in a state of semi-undress. There are suggestions Katherine was privy to this 'game' and she may well have been but chose to turn a blind eye to the 'innocent fun' but when she caught the pair in a secluded spot on the verge of kissing she decided Elizabeth had to go. How much Jane knew of what was going on we do not know, she was not in residence at the time of the scandal and there was never any suggestion he behaved in a similar manner with her, but if he had plans to marry her to Edward then Jane's credibility had to be beyond reproach. The treatment of Elizabeth by Seymour is nothing short of predatory. He appeared to be grooming her and his actions were so scandalous the Privy Council ordered an inquiry into what exactly had been going on at Chelsea. If he was to be found guilty of any improper conduct towards the princess then he may have found himself facing a charge of treason.

Katherine was pregnant at the time and the affair took its toll on the marriage so in order to build some bridges the couple decided to leave their London home and head for Seymour's country seat, Sudeley Castle in Gloucestershire where Katherine could prepare for the birth. Jane was back with the household at the time of the move and the decision was made that she would go with them to Sudeley, clearly her parents were not overly concerned by the rumours surrounding Seymour's behaviour and allowed her to stay under his care. Jane and Katherine were clearly close, Katherine had longed to be a mother and having Jane's company offered her the chance to release her maternal feelings and Jane, who had never been close to her mother, probably relished the closeness and motherly affection.

Jane had been living away from her parents for some time now and her father took the opportunity to visit his daughter when the family relocated from London to Bradgate for the summer. No doubt concerned about the rumours he had heard at court about Seymour's behaviour with Elizabeth, he needed to see for himself that Jane was being well cared for. In the August he made the seventy-mile trip from Leicestershire to see Jane at Sudeley, we can only assume he made the visit alone as there are no records of Frances or either of Jane's sisters accompanying him. Jane would no doubt have been pleased to see him, of her parents, it is her father she was closest to as they bonded over their religious beliefs, Frances never quite reached the same levels of fanaticism they did. The visit gave Henry the chance to assess how well his daughter was doing in her studies and to check on her behaviour. He would have been greeted by a happy young lady who was engaged in her work and settled in her homelife he would have been pleased at what he saw, although he may not have been so pleased to see a stubbornness developing in her character. He may have advised her to work on that before she met with her mother again. He brought news of her sisters, Katherine had begun to learn Greek with Thomas Harding, the family Chaplain at Bradgate and no doubt Mary was well engaged with her studies too, although her younger age meant she was far behind Jane.

But it wasn't just his daughter that Henry came to see when he visited Sudeley, visiting Jane made a good cover story to visit Thomas who was still smouldering over his snub by Somerset to restrict his power. Thomas decided it was time to take action. He was plotting and the binds that now tied Seymour and Dorset meant the naïve Henry had little choice but to help Seymour in his quest to try and oust the Lord Protector from power. Somerset, in his bid to have all encompassing control, had banned all access to the king which meant Seymour and Katherine could no longer visit Edward and drop poison in his ear over the tyrannic like grasp Somerset had over him. It was this snub which may have prompted them to up sticks and head for Sudeley, being in the country air was good for Katherine but it also meant Thomas could plot in secret away from court. But the lack of access to Edward must have rung alarm bells for Henry and Frances, they had been nurturing the idea of this marriage long before Seymour suggested it, but with access restricted how did Seymour propose to arrange the wedding between the king and Jane? The Greys had handed over the control of their prized eldest daughter based on the promise she would marry Edward and become queen, what should their next move be? Remove Jane from his care or hedge their bets and stick by him and his promises? Thomas was clear in his plan; he felt the king needed to be removed from the Lord Protector's grasp and asked Henry to go back to Bradgate and rally as many men as he could ready to march on London to free the king. Knowing what we do about Henry's character and his lack of common sense he no doubt readily offered all his support, but if he did waver, Thomas could always use the potential marriage between Edward and Jane as a leverage to gain his support.

Thomas's plans were thrown into chaos when Katherine Parr gave birth to a daughter named Mary, presumably named after the Lady Mary on 30 August 1548. Sadly, the former queen of England passed away from puerperal fever on 5 September, it is not thought Jane was present during or after the birth given her age but she was in residence at the time. Did she hear the anguished screams as Katherine toiled through labour followed by the mewling cries of a newborn baby? Knowing how close Jane was to Katherine she more than likely loitered near the birthing chamber door waiting for news. When the news reached her a few days later that Katherine had died she must have been devastated, not only had she lost her friend and mentor but with Seymour grief stricken she was suddenly without any guidance or support. Katherine had been a positive influence on Jane and it was probably as a result of their friendship that the future devout Jane was shaped.

Jane performed the role of chief mourner at Katherine's funeral which took place on 7 September at St Mary's Church which sits nestled in the grounds of Sudeley Castle. Her burial here makes her the only English queen to be buried on private land and her funeral is reported to have been the first Protestant funeral in England. It was a huge responsibility that had been placed on Jane's young shoulders but she was determined to do a good job for Katherine. She did not put a foot wrong and would have done her parents proud with her faultless behaviour throughout what can only have been a traumatic experience for the young girl clad head to toe in black. Following the service the mourners returned to the castle for dinner, where Jane sat and presided over what would have been a very sad meal. As the guests started to leave Jane had to wait for her fate to be decided.

With Katherine now gone, there was no female to head the household so it would not have been right and proper for her to stay in the company of a man with a questionable reputation. Eventually, in his grief, Seymour decided it would be best for Jane to return to her family at Bradgate with Frances and Henry agreeing that would be the best course of action. It had been an unsettling time and they must have been relieved to get their daughter back under their roof. Despite her grief at losing Katherine at least the uncertainty surrounding her future now appeared to be settled. At last Jane had a sense of relief and no doubt was pleased to be returning home to the familiar surroundings of Bradgate and her family. We do not know for certain what kind of relationship she had with her younger sisters but after months apart she must have been looking forward to seeing them again. Sadly, Jane would not know it at the time but those joyful and fulfilling months with Katherine would be the happiest of her short life. She had enjoyed the companionship of an intelligent, kind and caring woman, perhaps something she had not had the fortune of experiencing in her life. To think how different things may have been had Katherine lived long enough to guide Jane over the coming years, maybe Katherine would have offered counsel to Jane when she was faced with the news she was to be queen.

All appeared to be settled, Jane was ready to return to Bradgate but at the last minute as she prepared to make the journey home Seymour had a change of heart and decided it would be best if she stayed with him. Why the sudden change? Had the fog of his grief cleared and the realisation he was about to lose his prized asset dawned on him? He knew he had to work fast, Jane was ready for the off so he wrote to Frances and Henry explaining that he had been too hasty in making his decision and that Jane should stay with him, their original agreement still stood. But for a lady like Jane, it would be improper for her not to be under the care of a high-ranking female and with Katherine dead the only option available to Thomas was to suggest she enter the care of his mother Margery. Margery Seymour was the daughter of Sir Henry Wentworth and Anne Say and in 1494 she married prominent courtier Sir John Seymour. The couple set up home at Wulfhall in Wiltshire and had ten children together. Following the death of her husband in 1536 Margery decided to take a more active role in the lives of her children and grandchildren making her the perfect candidate to offer Jane a guiding hand. She would be responsible for Jane's welfare and would have to ensure she received adequate supervision when required. On the face of it this seemed like a reasonable offer, Jane liked Seymour and it was clear she was thriving under his care, she was settled in his household and it would be a shame for her to leave. Henry refused Seymour's offer and insisted that Jane return home to them. So, she set off for Bradgate and returned to her parents' home under the impression her future lay there with them.

The Greys expressed their gratitude to Seymour for everything he had done for their daughter in the eighteen months she had been with him but in reality the talk of marriage with the king had not materialised beyond anything but talk. Seymour's standing had changed with the death of Katherine, his influence at court had diminished even further and he was even more at odds with his brother the Lord Protector. Frances and Henry wrote to Seymour expressing their intentions regarding Jane's future but in order to keep in his good books they assured him they would still consult him over any future marriage proposals. This is a strange promise to make, it is not as though the Greys were a middle ranking noble family, Henry was Marquess of Dorset and Frances first cousin to the king so why does it appear they were so desperate to please Seymour? Did they still harbour hopes that he could arrange a marriage to the king or were they playing the long game, not overly committing themselves to either camp? At the end of the day, she was their daughter and Henry, as her father, was the one who would decide on her marriage, with the king's consent of course.

Katherine's death became an opportunity for Frances to resume control of her daughter's upbringing. How she felt about handing over her daughter in the first place is questionable as she would have liked to keep a grip on her future but she seemed very keen to have Jane back under her care at the earliest chance. Henry was 'fully determined, that his Daughter the Lady Jane should no more com to remain with the Lord Admiral' and both he and Frances had in their minds how their children ought to behave. When Jane returned home it did not take long for her parents to realise the child that had left eighteen months earlier was not the young lady that came home from Sudeley. Jane seemed to have become a spoilt and strong-willed young woman, traits which were not appreciated by her parents. She was also very intelligent with a questioning nature and was no longer willing to accept what she was told; she questioned the world around her and her place in it. She finally understood who she was and what was expected of her and no one could better train her than her mother who had lived the life of being the eldest daughter of prominent parents. Frances was the driving force behind Jane's return home and Henry was never really capable of negotiating a deal very well so his wife took control and demanded her daughter's return. Maybe Frances felt anxious that Jane was not being raised in the manner she thought was acceptable for a girl of her station and it appears she was right to be concerned. Regardless of how her parents felt over her behavioural changes it must have been a joy for Katherine and Mary to see their elder sister again, although the age gap must have felt even wider now, Jane had changed.

From Seymour's point of view, the letter he sent to Henry and Frances should have been enough to ensure that Jane was to stay with him, he had come through his grief and it had all been a big mistake to allow Jane to return home, but it was ok, he had sent a letter explaining the situation so all should be well. Jane was to unpack and forget everything that had happened, she was going nowhere. Well sadly, he was wrong, Henry, and in particular Frances, were not about to let their daughter go as easily as they had done before. As far as Seymour was concerned it was a done deal so he rather arrogantly decided to leave Jane at Sudeley whilst he travelled to London on business thinking he had the Greys hanging off his every word. Little did he know that as he travelled across country to London, Henry was on his way to Sudeley to collect his daughter to take her home to Bradgate. She finally arrived home at the end of September. Upon his arrival back at Sudeley, Seymour wrote to the Greys at Bradgate, his letter, dated 17 September reads:

> After my most hartye commend unto your good Lordship. Whereby my last lettres unto the same, written in a Tyme when partelye with the Quene's Deathe, I was so amased, that I had smale regard eyther to my self or to my doings; and partelye then thinking that my great losse must presently have constrained me to have broken upp and dissolved my hole house, I offred unto your Lordship to send mt Lady Jane unto you,whensoever you wolde sende for her,as to him whome I thought wolde be most tendre on hir; Forasmuche as sithens being bothe better advised of my self, and having more depelye disgested whereunto my Power wolde extend; I fynde indeed that with God's helpe, I shall right well be hable to contynewe my House together, without dyminisheng any greate parte therof. And therefore putting my hole Affyance and Trust in God have begonne of newe to establish my Houshold, where shall remayne not oonlye the Gentlewomen of the Quene's Hieghnes Privey Chamber, but also the Maids which wayted at larg, and other Women being about her Grace in her life Tyme, with a hundred and twenty Gentlemen and Yeomen, conynualle abeyding in House together; saving that now presentlye certaine of the Mayds and Gentlemen have desired to have Licence for a Moneth, or such a thing, to see theyr Friends; and then immediately returne hither again. And therfore doubting, least your Lordship might think any unkindness, that I should by my saide lettres take occasion to rydd me of your Doughter so soon after the Quenes Death: For the Prof both of my hartye Affection towards youe, and good Will towards hir, I mynd bow to keape her, until I shall next speak with your Lordshipp; whiche should have been within these thre or four days,

if it had not been that I must repayr unto Corte, aswell to help certane of the Quenes pore Servants, with some of the Things now fallen bt her Death, as also for my owne Affayrs; oneles I shalbe advertised from your Lordship of your expresse Mynd to the contrarye. My Ladye, mt Mother, shall and wooll, I doubt not, be as deare unto hir, as though hir owne Doughter. And for my owne Parte, I shall contynewe her haulf Father and more; and all that are in my House shall be as diligent about her, as your self wolde wyshe accordinglye.

He clearly admits to being too hasty in dismissing Katherine's household and now he had had time to think on it he decided Jane should return to him. When the letter arrived at Bradgate, Jane was made to reply directly to Seymour herself, she insisted she was happy to be back with her parents and thanked him for all he had done for her, her letter read:

My duty to your Lordship in most humble wise remembered, with no less thanks for the gentle letters which I received from you. Thinking myself so much bound to your Lordship, for your great goodness towards me from time to time, that I cannot by any means be able to recompense the least part thereof, I purposed to write a few rude lines unto your Lordship, rather as a token to show how much worthier I think your Lordship's goodness than to give worthy thanks for the same; and these my letters shall be to testify unto you that, like as you have become towards me a loving and kind father, so I shall be always most ready to obey your godly monitions and good instructions, as becometh one upon whom you have heaped so many benefits. And thus, fearing lest I should trouble your Lordship too much, I most humbly take my leave of your good Lordship.

Your humble servant during my life
Jane Grey

Henry also replied to Seymour's letter stating that it would be better for Jane if she was to stay now in the care of her mother, he thanked him for all he had done for his daughter, he explained:

My most hartie Comendations unto your good Lordship not forgotten. Wher it hath pleased yow by your most gentle Lettres to offre me thabode of my Doughter at your Lordefhypes House, I do as well acknoledge your most frendly Affection towards me and hyr herin, as also rendre unto yow most deferv'd thanks for the fame: Nevertheless considering the State of my Doughter and hyr tendre Yeres, (wherin she shall hardlie rule hyr fylfe as yet without a Guide, left she shuld for lacke of a Bridle, tak to moche the Head, and conceave such Opinion of hyr fylfe, that all such good behauior as she heretofore hath learned, by the Quenes and your most holsom instructions, shuld either altogither be quenched in hyr, or at the lefte moche diminished, I shall in most hartie wise require your Lordcfhippe to committ hyr to the Governance of hyr Mother; by whom for the Feare and Duetie she owithe hyr, she shall most easlye be rulid and framid towards Vcrtuc, which I wishe above all Things to be most plentifull in hyr

And although your Lordships good Mynd, concerning hyr honest and godlie Education, is so great, that myn can be no more; yet waying, that yow be destitute of suche one as shuld corredte hyr as a Mystres, and monishe hyr as a Mother, I perswade my sylfe that yow wyl think the Eye and Overfight of my Wife shalbe in thys respedt most necefsarie. My Meaning herin ys not to withdrawe anie Parte of my Promise to yow for hyr bestowing; for I assure your Lordship, I intend, God wylling, to use your discrete Advise and Consent in that behalfe, and no lesse then myn own: Onlye I seeke in thes hyr yonge Yeres, wherin she now standeth, either to make or marre (as the common saing ys) thadressing of hyr Mynd to Humilytye, Sobrenes, and Obedience. Wherfore looking upon that fatherlie Affection which yow beare hyr, my truste is, that your good Lordship waying the Premisses, wylbe content to charge hyr Mother with hyr, whofe waking Eye in respecting hyr demeanor shalbe, I hope, no lesse, then yow as a Frend, and I as a Father wuld wishe. And thus wishing your Lordship a perfitght ryddaunce of all Unquietnes and Greife of Mynd. I have anie further to trouble your Lordship.

But Seymour was a persistent man and he knew what a loss Jane would be to his bigger plans so he decided to visit Bradgate with his friend Sir William Sharington and between them they plotted to work on Henry and Frances. They decided to divide and conquer, Sharington took on Frances and managed to wear her down. Whilst Seymour took Henry aside and reminded him of what great things his family could achieve if they allowed Jane to return to his care.

Surprisingly, Seymour was still making the bold claim that he could arrange the marriage between the king and Jane. But maybe this was a more believable plan than we give him credit for especially as Mary, Queen of Scots had gone to France to marry the Dauphin. It had been a long-held desire that she would come south to England to be Edward's bride and unite the two countries under one crown but the Scots had resisted any English requests and the two countries had fought a bitter war for eight years over the marriage of their queen. The 'Rough Wooing' had forced Scotland to look to France for a husband for their young queen and so she sailed away right under the noses of the English forces. But the news was not all bad, especially for Thomas, as it meant the search for a bride for Edward was back on and had been blown wide open.

Henry and Frances finally gave in to Seymour's demands and Jane returned to his care but not before they had managed to negotiate a further payment of £500 from him and a renewed promise of marriage to the king. So, Jane was packing up again and by the end of October, she was back in London at Seymour Place where she entered the care of Lady Seymour, Thomas's aged mother. It seems that sending Jane back to Seymour was not a decision they took lightly, his behaviour had started to become erratic and without Katherine's steadying hand who knew what he was capable of. He was also openly plotting against his brother, fed up of being ignored he felt as the king's uncle he too deserved a say in matters of state, but he was too unpredictable. He was flirting with danger and when rumours started circulating that he planned to marry the Lady Elizabeth the council sat up and took notice. Henry and Frances were strongly advised to remove Jane from his care, but they recklessly ignored all the warnings. Seymour's downfall was going to be spectacular and the Greys had positioned themselves in the middle of the potential fallout. They were going to need to distance themselves as quickly as possible if they were to dodge suspicion' but the ever-naive Henry Grey stuck by his ill-fated friend until even he knew it was time to jump ship.

As plans go, this was a pretty bad one. Seymour was plotting to kidnap the young king, his own nephew, from his bedchamber at Hampton Court Palace. He planned to steal away with him in the night, taking him out of the evil clutches of his wicked uncle Somerset. Once he had him safely ensconced at Windsor, he would arrange the wedding between Jane and Edward and no doubt he would try and rule the country through them. On the night in question Edward's guard was woken by a dog barking outside the king's door and raised the alarm. In a panic, Seymour shot the dog and fled the scene before any harm to the king could be made. Everyone knew it was Seymour that had attempted the kidnap and he was summoned to appear before the Privy Council the very next day. He refused, so the guards came knocking at Seymour Place where he was arrested. We can only assume Jane was in residence at the time but how much she knew of the reasoning behind his arrest we simply do not know.

Thomas Seymour's arrest sent shockwaves through the court and as soon as Henry and Frances heard the news they did their upmost to disassociate themselves from him, if they didn't they risked being dragged into the dangerous political quagmire and the deadly risks that came with it. In order to prove his allegiance to the king, and to remove any slight hint of treason, Henry turned his back on his one-time friend, guardian of his daughter, and agreed to give evidence against Seymour. When questioned, Seymour told the council of his plans to remove the king from the clutches of the Lord Protector and that he had bullied and coerced the Greys into letting Jane stay in his care, with the view to marrying Edward to her.

The net spread wide and Sharington's home was raided and his fraudulent activities at the Royal Mint exposed. But when questioned, he insisted he knew nothing more of any plot other than of his marrying the Lady Elizabeth. Interestingly, that was a rumour that was confirmed by many of those interrogated by the Privy Council but was one she denied, she even had to go as far as denying that she had fallen pregnant by him. When it came to Henry's evidence he did not hold back and he contributed to Seymour being found guilty of high treason. For reasons unknown he was denied a public trial and the Act of Attainder was passed against him. He was sentenced to death and was executed on 20 March 1549 on Tower Hill. Not much is known about the fate of his young daughter Mary, with both her parents dead she would more than likely have been taken in by relatives but there is no evidence to suggest what happened to her. On the face of it, it appears Seymour was not necessarily executed for what he had done in terms of harming the king, which was not his aim, but more for what he could do in the future. He posed a threat to his brother and that threat had to be eliminated, it was difficult for Edward to sign the death warrant of his favourite uncle and no doubt Somerset leaned on him to do so. This whole affair is the first example of Henry placing his daughter in potentially dangerous situations, he was lucky those prosecuting Seymour took his giving evidence as a means of extricating himself from the situation, otherwise the consequences could have been disastrous.

Thomas Seymour played an important and almost father like role in Jane's upbringing. He encouraged her education, supported her religious choices and made plans for her future. He saw, before anyone else did, just how valuable she was in the marriage market and he would not be the last to do so. He was also the first man to exploit this young girl in order to grasp power for himself, again, he would not be the last to do so. Seymour was canny because he knew that by having Jane in his household no one else could have access to her, no one else could have any control over her and even her parents, to some degree, were removed from Jane's immediate future. He also knew how much having the third in line to the throne would upset and frustrate his brother the Lord Protector and any one-upmanship he could get over him was important. Thomas was thinking long term, he knew Somerset would look upon Jane as a potential bride for his eldest son, Lord Hertford but with Jane a potential target for Edward meant Seymour had leverage to lure the young king away from the clutches of his brother and into his own care. Jane and Edward were of a similar age and by all accounts got on well, the young king must have craved company of his own age rather than just his councillors. From Jane's perspective she seems to have enjoyed her time under Seymour's care, especially when Katherine was alive, even after her death she did not seem in a rush to return home. His death would no doubt have had a profound effect on her young mind but it was time once again to return home to her family and to her studies.

Chapter 6

Marriage to a King?

By September 1549 it would seem any lingering doubt there may have been over Henry's involvement with Seymour had vanished as the Greys were in high favour with the king. Edward visited the family at Dorset House where a feast and entertainment was laid on for him to enjoy, no doubt Jane was present as it was too good of an opportunity to miss. There is no clear evidence to suggest Edward and Jane spent much time together as children, some suggest they were educated together when they were younger and had built up a firm friendship but others indicate their meetings were few and far between. Regardless of what had gone before, the get together at Dorset House was an ideal time for the two cousins to get to know each other. With Seymour now dead the plan to marry the pair seemed to lay in tatters, did that dream die with him or did Henry and Frances hope to engineer the match themselves? Surely they still held aspirations for a marriage between the pair for they were ambitious for their children, especially Jane who up to this point had shown so much promise. The best way for them to remind Edward that his young English, intelligent and religiously fanatical cousin existed was to be around him as much as possible. With Henry now seemingly in favour he spent much of his time in attendance on the king which in turn led to Frances and the sisters spending more time at court than ever before.

The proposed marriage between Edward and Jane is an interesting one. Certainly no one would have asked Jane if she desired a marriage with the king and there is no evidence to suggest they ever harboured any romantic feelings for each other and with Edward still being under his majority age he would perhaps have not been in any position to force a union. Any potential marriage of Edwards attracted huge interest across Europe and foreign ambassadors were in constant discussion over which royal house Edward would choose to marry into. The courtiers would have been the ones to suggest potential brides and they would have been looking for a foreign allegiance to build relations and bolster England's depleted treasury. The Marquess of Northampton was sent to France to negotiate such a match. The initial plan was to lure Mary, Queen of Scots back but there was no way the French would give up that prize so instead the eldest daughter of Henri II, Elisabeth de Valois, was suggested as a potential bride. She was only six years old at the time but that would give the young couple time to get to know each other before they became of marriageable age. She was described as being pretty and of having a sweet nature albeit a shy one. Edward was urged to make the match by his councillors, an alliance with France meant the two countries could unite against the Holy Roman Empire whose leader was Charles V, cousin to the Lady Mary which is why the negotiations were conducted with the upmost secrecy. After much cajoling Edward agreed and the French ambassadors arrived in London to finalise the details. Of course, the news leaked out and was soon the only topic of conversation at court. Foreign matches were often preferred not only for the benefit of peace and trade but as we had seen in the past, with the Seymour and the Boleyn families, an English family can get above its station when a daughter marries a king. Members of the council would not have wanted a rival family to assume power over them so it was safer to negotiate abroad.

But if a marriage with France was on the cards where did that leave Henry and Frances and their hopes for Jane? It would seem that dream had died with Thomas Seymour but little did they know bigger things were on the horizon for their daughter. Of course, it would have been a coup for the Greys if their eldest daughter had married Edward, he brought wealth, power and a crown, but what if Jane assumed the crown all for herself? When they heard the news that Edward's marriage with Elisabeth was no longer on the cards they must have renewed their hope that Jane was once again in the frame.

As ever at the Tudor court no one could rest on their laurels and with Thomas Seymour now dead, his brother would have naively thought his position as Lord Protector was now stable, but that was not the case. The council were starting to see his faults and began opposing his rule and the southern uprisings would prove to be the final nail in the Protector's coffin. It was felt Somerset had shown too much leniency towards the rebels, despite being warned by his onetime supporter William Paget to be stronger he ignored this and before long the nobles began to lose faith in him. Paget had been one of Somerset's biggest supporters at the beginning of his protectorship but the duke's inability to take counsel from others was proving to be too dictatorial for Paget to continue to support, it would appear Somerset was just as stubborn as his younger brother.

Before his death, Thomas had planted a seed in the counsellors heads that the Lord Protector was starting to lose his grip on the king. Somerset was continuing to treat him as a child but he was now 12 years old, which in Tudor England was not young, and his constant meddling and molly-coddling was starting to grate on Edward, leading him to resent his uncle's grip on him. Edward's desire for more freedom soon made the lords of the council restless and before long they were plotting to confront Somerset at Hampton Court Palace. He had heard the rumours and decided to move Edward to Windsor for safety, although whose safety he was concerned about is questionable. On the face of it the Protector's intentions were honourable, he was merely looking out for the welfare of his nephew and king but Edward was beginning to feel like a prisoner and with no power to change his situation he started to pull further away from him. It must have been a frustrating time for the king, he was desperate to exert his power but was stifled at every turn, he was a clever child and was always keen to remind people he was king but he was still too young to take the full reins of power. The Lords must have sensed the king's unhappiness and decided to act. On 11 October the Lord Protector was arrested and imprisoned in the Tower of London. Henry backed the council in their actions, as always he was keen to be seen to be supporting the right side, he had helped condemn one Seymour brother to death, he clearly had no qualms in sending another to the block.

The arrest and imprisonment of Somerset proved to be far more beneficial to Henry than he could have ever expected, he was finally elected to the Privy Council. Henry had spent many years being ignored on the political front, he never really advanced under Henry VIII and Edward had shown little interest but finally he had his place amongst the most powerful men in the country. Knowing what we do of Henry's character it is not surprising to learn that he did not become a frequent attendee at the meetings. On the face of it he comes across as a man that liked the prestige a position could bring him but when it came down to the nitty gritty of doing the work he was perhaps not as enthusiastic as he ought to have been. Along with the appointment to the council came wealth and power and to boost his coffers he was appointed Constable of Leicestershire, Rutland, Nottinghamshire and Warwickshire.

Edward was still too young to rule by himself and with Somerset in the tower a gap emerged for the role of Protector. Initially, Thomas Wriothesley, 1st Earl of Southampton, took charge on an interim basis but it would take until October 1551 before a more permanent person was elected to fill that role. The man who filled that gap was John Dudley, Earl of Warwick. John Dudley was born in 1504, his father, Edmund Dudley had been a minister to Henry VII but was later executed by Henry VIII in 1510 for his supposed inappropriate financial dealings. The execution of his father led to John Dudley joining the household of Sir Edward Guildford as his ward aged 7 years old. It was here he met his future wife Jane Guildford, Sir Edward's daughter. The couple married in 1525 and had thirteen children together, including the favourite of Elizabeth I, Lord Robert. It seems to have been a happy and loving marriage. It would appear the son did not suffer for the sins of the father as Dudley rose high during the reign of Henry VIII becoming the deputy governor general of Calais in 1538 and later Lord High Admiral in 1542. He inherited the title of Viscount Lisle through his mother which elevated him to the lower ranks of the nobility. He was a well-respected soldier having served in many successful campaigns against the Scots and French which led to peace. He climbed the ranks of nobility further when he was created Earl of Warwick in 1546 by Edward VI. Henry VIII must have held him in the highest regards as he made him one of the sixteen members of the regency council to guide Edward through his early reign. But he had finally had enough of Somerset's dictatorship and became an instrumental voice in his ultimate downfall. Somerset was eventually released from the tower and was pardoned by his nephew, he was even allowed to re-join the council but in a much less powerful role and was made to understand that he was no longer in charge.

As always, life in London was tumultuous so Frances and her daughters travelled to Essex to spend the Christmas season at Tilty Abbey with her family. Tilty Abbey had been a Cistercian monastery up until 1535 when it was dissolved as part of the dissolution under Henry VIII. After which it was passed over to Thomas Audley, 1st Baron Audley of Waldon, the husband of Jane's aunt Elizabeth. Whilst they were staying at Tilty they travelled just under twenty miles on to the Palace of Beaulieu to visit Frances's cousin the Lady Mary. Beaulieu, meaning beautiful place, had been granted to Mary following the death of her father and remained one of her favourite residences. It was a grand palace which boasted the traditional Tudor style gatehouse, set around a central courtyard. There were multiple rooms which were richly decorated and probably its most attractive feature was its location. It was close to London should Mary be required but at the same time far enough way for her to be out of Edwards reach.

Mary was not in the best of health during this time, she had been suffering depression for some years and would not have been at ease with herself whilst she remained at odds with her brother over religion. The constant quarrels with Edward had somewhat alienated Mary from court and no doubt a visit from her cousin brought some cheer to the Christmas period. Frances and Mary had always been close so this was a trip everyone looked forward to. Jane and Mary were on opposite sides of the religious spectrum and both were equally fanatical in their respective beliefs. Jane had already shown how fervent she was in her reformist beliefs and Mary had openly defied the king and the council in maintaining her catholic masses. She had six chaplains in her household and no amount of cajoling would make her change that and she defiantly continued to hear mass in all her homes. Mary's persistent breaking of the rules angered the Privy Council and as Henry was a strict evangelical he claimed she should not be left in peace for as long as she remained a catholic. It would seem to Frances that her whole family was set against her cousin, but she always remained on good terms with her and that loyalty would prove invaluable in the years to come. So perhaps it was inevitable Mary and Jane were going to clash at some point, two fiery Tudor women with strong opinions could only result in confrontation.

At some point during the stay Jane was shown to the chapel by one of Mary's ladies. We are led to believe this was Lady Anne Wharton and when she entered the chapel she paused and genuflected at the altar. Jane enquired if Mary was in the chapel and was astonished when Lady Wharton said she curtseyed 'to Him that made us all'. Lady Wharton was taken aback by Jane's rude questioning of her. Jane was utterly incredulous and simply could not understand why had she done this, in her eyes it was a preposterous thing to do! She was openly rude and insolent towards Lady Anne and when Mary heard of her outburst she declared Jane had not only insulted Anne but her and her catholic household as well. Jane was a guest of Mary and would have been expected to behave in a certain way but she showed no manners whatsoever and the relationship between the two suddenly became strained and difficult.

There are doubts over whether or not this incident did in fact take place, but if it did, it gives us a clear indication just how fanatical Jane had become in her religious beliefs. She was bordering on arrogance and displaying a complete lack of understanding, she couldn't comprehend that people thought differently to her. Jane should have taken a leaf out of her mother's book, Frances and Mary had always been close, regardless of their differing religious beliefs they had managed to maintain a respectful, friendly and caring relationship which Jane had now put at risk through her childish outburst. One can only imagine how Frances felt at her impetuous daughter's behaviour towards her cousin. She must have been furious and embarrassed, Mary had welcomed them into her home and she had displayed nothing but rudeness, one can only assume Frances was very displeased. On the other hand, Henry would probably have applauded his daughters outburst, congratulating her on her mockery of the catholic faith and more importantly, of Mary.

The relationship between Frances and Jane has often been described as tense and at times even violent and whilst violence cannot and should not be tolerated or used as a means of punishment, it is understandable how Frances became frustrated with her eldest daughter. She had put much effort into making sure her children were brought up correctly, ensuring they were well educated for girls of their station and yet Jane had developed a ruthless streak to her. Henry and Frances had always been strict parents and were clear on how their daughters, and Jane in particular, should be behaving. In Jane lay the future of the family and they could not allow her to ruin her chances with bad behaviour. But let's not put all the blame on Jane, she was a young girl trying to find her feet in the world, yes she was opinionated when it came to religion but that does not make her a bad person or even a naughty child. Maybe if Frances and Henry had kept her in their household instead of selling her off to Seymour, which let's face it is what they did, they would have no complaints to make over her behaviour.

Views on Frances and Henry's parenting techniques come mainly from one source when on one occasion Roger Ascham paid a visit to Bradgate only to find Henry and Frances were out hunting in the grounds. To his surprise he found Jane was at home, she greeted him politely yet he wondered why she had not joined her parents and sisters out on the hunt. She explained she was happier to be sat with her books, 'all their sport in the park is but a shadow to that pleasure that I find in Plato'. She found such solace in reading her books and her Greek texts proved to be much more of a challenge and much more stimulating than riding and hunting. Ascham was surprised to see that she was reading at such an advance stage for her age, but at the same time understood she was the kind of girl that found more pleasure in her books than in anything else life had to offer. Her commitment to her books shows us just how serious a girl she was. Jane had never been a frivolous or fancy kind of girl but her reading of these texts had made her strong willed and single minded, traits her parents were not keen on. Henry and Frances saw Jane's behaviour as being defiant and wilful and it has been a long-held belief that her parents resorted to violence in an attempt to steer her down the path they felt she should be on. Some reports indicate they beat her regularly in an attempt to get her to yield to their views. Jane was stubborn and would always stand up for her beliefs, she would defy her parents but only when she truly believed she was in the right. Sadly, for Jane, and for many other girls in her position, her sole purpose in life was to attract a wealthy and powerful husband who could bring great riches to the family. Jane made a rather bold statement to Ascham regarding her feelings towards her parents in which she backs the claims of abuse up:

> One of the greatest benefits that ever God gave me is that He sent me so sharp and severe parents and so gentle a schoolmaster. For when I am in presence either of father or mother, whether I speak, keep silence, sit, stand, or go, eat, drink, be merry or sad, be sewing, playing, dancing or doing anything else, I must do it, as it were, in such weight, measure, and number, even so perfectly as God made the world, or else I am so sharply taunted, so cruelly threatened, yea, presently sometimes with pinches, nips, and bobs and other ways which I will not name for the honour I bear them.

She then goes on to say how much joy she gets from her lessons with Aylmer, he is gentle and kind to her yet when she is called from her studies she falls 'on weeping because whatsoever I do else but learning is full of grief, trouble, fear, and whole misliking unto me.' You can feel her heartbreak from the page, here is a young girl with so much expectation on her shoulders and all she wanted to do was be with her books.

From our modern-day perspective, we often presume relationships in the sixteenth century between children and their parents were much more distant and unemotional, especially in the upper classes and a child being struck by a parent was not unusual or frowned upon as it is today. Even though there are reports of these beatings from Ascham, there are no other contemporary accounts to confirm this behaviour and indeed there is no evidence at all to suggest any of the Grey sisters were physically abused by either parent. Therefore, the declaration should be taken at face value. There is no denying that Frances and Henry were strict parents but this reference to Jane being beaten by her parents was only printed in 1570, long after those involved had died and long after they could defend themselves against any accusation. If what Ascham has described here is true then one can only feel heartache for Jane for the abuse she was forced to endure as a child. It makes for truly distressing reading and even though it was not uncommon for children at this time to receive a beating if they stepped out of line, it would appear Jane lived in constant fear of her parents. They were clearly looking for absolute perfection from their eldest daughter, and no person can deliver that all of the time, how could she ever say no to them if this was the punishment meted out to her. It was from this declaration that Frances's image developed as a cruel and evil mother who had no maternal inclination and who was never close to her daughter. She is often described as forceful, a woman who had dynastic ambitions for her family. She liked to get her own way and was never to be gainsaid. Frances was the head of her household and she ruled them and her family in an almost tyrannical manner. This enduring image of Frances's character has been tainted ever since thanks to this passage and it continues to this day thanks to modern day interpretations of Jane's life. The story is slightly different when it comes to her father. They had a much closer relationship due to a shared religious fanaticism that bonded them.

The family spent the Christmas of 1549 together at Tilty and despite Jane's run-in with Mary there was much to celebrate. The invitation extended to the wider family and friends of Henry and Frances and there was plenty to eat at the feasts and banquets, and much enjoyment was taken from the plays and masques that were performed in the great hall. The Grey sisters more than likely put on a special performance, Katherine and Mary were fun and frivolous but Jane was much more serious so her role may have been less cheerful but it is perhaps unfair to assume Jane was a dour young girl who did not know how to have fun. With sisters like Katherine and Mary it would have been hard not to get carried away with the festivities but to Jane the religious aspect of Christmas would have outweighed the jovial festivities.

In February 1551, much to his dismay, Henry was named Lord Warden of the North Marches, this was a government office that was responsible for the security along the English/Scottish border. It would have been Henry's job to quell any Scottish threat and command any military action that was deemed necessary. He headed north in the April but sadly only lasted until the September when John Dudley had to take over given Henry's lack of ability. Why he was chosen for this post is questionable given his lack of military experience and lack of desire to work at all and it is almost certainly a role he did not relish. He would have had little choice in the matter as it was on the king's orders so he set off for Berwick in the north-east of the country. When he arrived, he quickly realised the soldiers were under paid and funds were urgently needed if they were to stand any chance of holding off a Scottish attack. He made continuous complaints to the council on behalf of the troops for monetary assistance but his pleas fell on deaf ears. It was clear the council wanted him to do the job quietly and the constant complaints coupled with his lack of military talent failed to impress and he was removed from his post. No doubt he was pleased to leave and head back south to his family, who had been staying at Bradgate during his absence.

Things were moving fast at court; John Dudley, the Earl of Warwick had been elected the new Lord Protector and to go along with his new role he also become the Duke of Northumberland. In the same ceremony on 11 October 1551 Henry was elevated to become the Duke of Suffolk. In a tragic twist of fate Frances's half-brothers Henry, Duke of Suffolk and Lord Charles caught the sweating sickness and died within an hour of each other on 14 July 1551, Henry had been 15 years old and his brother just 13. They had been residing at St John's College, Cambridge when the epidemic began to spread, the two brothers were brought to the Bishop of Lincoln's Palace in the small village of Buckden where it was considered safe. Sadly, Henry died first followed by his brother just an hour later. A joint funeral was held for the two boys which took place on 22 September. Their deaths left their mother Katherine Willoughby devastated and brought to an end the male line of the Brandon family plunging the dukedom of Suffolk into dormancy. Ordinarily a daughter would not automatically inherit a dukedom from her father but in this case Edward VI decided to confer the title on Frances thereby making her the Duchess of Suffolk, her husband took the title of Duke in the right of his wife.

Frances herself would also suffer with this terrible illness in 1552 but thankfully became one of the few to survive. It must have been severe and her life thought to have been in grave danger because as soon as Henry heard of his wife's illness he left court immediately to return to the family home at Charterhouse. It is thought the sisters were in residence at the time and Jane and the rest of family came to be by her bedside thinking she would not live much longer; it was clear Frances was suffering from a very serious illness. Thankfully she made a full recovery but this would have been a very worrying time for the family as she had always been the driving force behind the family. Her reputation of cruelty and hardness even spread to the treatment of her husband and as Frances got older many believed she became just as ruthless and cruel as her Uncle Henry. But again, this is not a contemporary vision of Frances and modern historians believe she has been misrepresented.

The Dukes of Suffolk and Northumberland were now working closely together and before long their fates would become so intertwined that events got so big neither of them could handle the catastrophic fallout, but that was in the future, for now Northumberland was keen to get to work with the King. However, things were about to get much worse for another duke. Despite his earlier release from the Tower of London and reinstatement to the council, Somerset now stood accused of wanting to overthrow the governorship of Northumberland. He was thrown into the tower on a charge of treason. Many believed this charge was a trumped-up attempt to finally remove Somerset from having any influence over his nephew, the king. The charge of treason would not stick so he was found guilty of a felony instead. A felony charge was a serious crime that carried the penalty of death and meant his estates would be confiscated and returned to the crown. Suffolk was present at the trial and he calmy watched on as the sentence of death was passed, Somerset was executed on 22 January 1552. King Edward marked the death of his uncle by claiming 'the duke of Somerset had his head cut off upon Tower Hill between eight and nine o'clock in the morning'. The young king had now signed the death warrants of two of his uncles, he was clearly his father's son and did not baulk at getting rid of those who caused him problems.

The death of Somerset and the conferring of the dukedom on Henry meant the fortunes of the Suffolks rose quickly. They naturally took over Suffolk Place which sat on the south side of the Thames near Winchester Palace and they used this for when they were required to be at court but they also took over the Charterhouse at Sheen which they made their main London family home. Northumberland was not as ostentatious as Somerset, he decided not to take the grand title of Lord Protector, instead he opted for Lord President of the Council. What he did do though was to include the king in the running of his country. Edward had always been a king that wanted his say, regardless of his young age. So, Northumberland's approach was to take what Edward had to say seriously but not having the familial link made him more wary in his dealings. He offered Edward a place at all the council meetings, Somerset had kept him away from government but now he was old enough and respected enough to be involved. The young king thrived under Northumberland's direction which led to the two forging a close and caring relationship. The king would take no action on any matter without seeking Northumberland's advice first and the two spent much time in consultation with each other.

Whilst her parents enjoyed their new status Jane continued her education and soon became a correspondent of the renowned Swiss theologian Henrich Bullinger. Bullinger was an ardent reformer, he led the Church of Zurich and became one of the Reformation's most influential men corresponding with leaders across Europe. Jane was encouraged by a man called John of Ulm to make contact with Bullinger. Ulm was German and had been exiled for his religious beliefs and Suffolk had taken him in at Bradgate and from there he became an acquaintance of Jane's. Again, it was thanks to her father's firm religious beliefs and his mixing in these circles that brought men like Bullinger into Jane's world and she thrived on corresponding with them about religion. They offered her an outlet, a safe space to set down her own understandings and beliefs and they never once belittled or ridiculed her, in fact she soon became so well renowned people sought her out.

Religion was the strongest bond Jane had with her father and he encouraged her when it came to expressing her views, even to men like Bullinger. He clearly had the confidence that his daughter could hold her own against such men. Her astounding intellect and ability to hold a rational debate was fast gaining her a reputation, she was seen, along with her father, as being leading reformists and not just in England, with connections like Bullinger her reputation was now stretching across Europe. Interacting with men like Bullinger led to a thirst for more knowledge, Jane was always looking for a way to widen her intellectual horizons so she decided to learn Hebrew with her tutors but her wealth of knowledge did not lead to an improvement of her manners and once again it was the Lady Mary that bore the brunt of her abruptness.

In November 1551 Jane was to attend the state visit of Marie de Guise, who was stopping off in London on her way back to Scotland after visiting her daughter Mary, Queen of Scots in France. She had decided to make the journey back to Scotland over land and was invited by Edward to attend his court. On the 5 November, Suffolk and the Earl of Huntingdon waited upon Marie at Baynard's Castle, the following day Frances was part of a contingent of ladies who accompanied Marie to court. In a bid to build bridges, the Lady Mary, who did not attend the festivities, kindly sent Jane a beautiful gown of cloth of gold to wear. Unfortunately, Jane did not appreciate the dress and did not go about declining the gift in a polite manner. 'What shall I do with it?' she petulantly asked. Maybe she felt it too grand for her to wear, or maybe it was the sender she had issues with. Either way she decided the gown did not suit her reserved, sober and rather serious person and refused point blank to wear it. You can imagine the disappointment her parents felt when they discovered Jane had tossed the gown to one side in defiance, no doubt they were disgusted by her behaviour. They felt their daughter's attitude was rude and insolent, it was simply an act of kindness from the Lady Mary, a present from one family member to another and could have been dealt with in a politer manner. But for Jane it was much more than the appearance of a dress. Mary was a catholic and Jane could not be seen to be receiving gifts from a catholic. From the outside looking in it appears Jane struggled with knowing how to deal with someone she came across who did not conform to her beliefs. Her attitude came across as being ignorant and just plain rude but by this stage she was too far down the reformist rabbit hole to be rational towards others. It was clear she wanted the persona of someone who was a devout evangelical, someone who never put a step wrong and someone who religion mattered before anything else. Was she beginning to take her religious fanaticism too far?

Chapter 7

An Unexpected Marriage

King Edward VI was not the pale and sickly child that history would have us remember him as. He was athletic and enjoyed many sports including hunting and jousting he was authoritative and full of his own self-importance. He expected to be obeyed on all matters, especially religion, regardless of his age he was king and his ministers, courtiers and subjects were expected to adopt his changes, and that included the Lady Mary. Her continuing defiance vexed him greatly which damaged their relationship and soon a distance began to materialise. He was definitely growing up in the mould of his father, in her book *Tudor England, A History*, Lucy Wooding talks of Edward not tolerating 'implied slights upon his majesty'. This is an important point to consider when thinking about his placing Jane as his heir, for if he was all of these things described above then surely he would not be easily cajoled into making amendments to the succession. He would name his heir and it would be his choice alone. Unfortunately for Edward as things stood there was no legitimate male Tudor heir for him to select. But as 1553 dawned the king fell ill, his symptoms included a hacking cough and a high fever and not many held out much hope he would live much longer, it was clear he was dying. The premature death of the king meant he would have to deal with the succession as a matter of urgency. Clearly not happy with the suggestions made by his father for the throne to pass to Mary, Edward decided to make drastic changes. News of the severity of the kings illness was kept quiet so as not to cause alarm, a succession crisis was not what the country needed but the Suffolks were at court awaiting news and Northumberland was ready to make his move.

It was clear to everyone that Edward was not going to marry and have an heir so steps had to be made to ensure the succession was as smooth a transition as possible. The problem Edward faced was that all the claimants were women and England had never been ruled by a queen regnant. Many queen consorts had been popular, Katherine of Aragon for example and Edward's grandmother Elizabeth of York had performed her role exceptionally well as consort to Henry VII, but having a queen actually ruling was a whole other matter. By the will of Henry VIII, his eldest daughter Mary, from his marriage with Katharine of Aragon, would become queen in her own right. There was an age gap of twenty-one years between Mary and Edward and their relationship was strained, but when they met at Whitehall she could not have been anything other than concerned and distressed to see how ill her younger brother had become.

Did she leave the palace after that visit wondering how long it would be before she was named queen? Northumberland certainly treated her like she was a queen in waiting but unfortunately for Mary, he had other ideas. The plan was that Mary was to be excluded from the succession due to her staunch Catholicism and her close familial links to Spain and the Holy Roman Empire, one of England's biggest rivals. Edward knew she would undo all his reforms if she was named queen so he was happy to omit her but that still left the issue of the Lady Elizabeth. She had been named in Henry VIII's will after Mary, if Northumberland wanted to cling to his power he would have to come up with a legitimate reason to exclude her too it would not do to exclude Mary and let Elizabeth remain, it would not work.

The reason they came up with was the fact she had been declared illegitimate and that alone forced Elizabeth out of the queue for the crown. Henry VIII had tarnished both his daughters with the stain of illegitimacy and despite restoring their right to the throne he did not reverse his decision on their legitimacy and that was enough for Northumberland to cast doubt over their eligibility. With that problem solved things were starting to move fast but he needed more time to put his plan into action. He decided to move Edward out of London to the cleaner air of Greenwich all the while attempting to deflect questions regarding the king's health. Mary and Elizabeth were now unwelcome at the palace, access to their brother was removed, surely that must have raised further concerns that Northumberland was up to something.

So, if Edward/Northumberland were planning to exclude Mary and Elizabeth, what options did that leave Edward when naming his successor? Well, as previously discussed Frances and her sister Eleanor had already been excluded by Henry VIII, on grounds we do not fully understand. Eleanor had died in 1547 leaving just one daughter, Margaret Clifford who was aged 13 at the time of Edward's death. At no point did Frances seem to challenge the decision to exclude her from the succession, in her mind Mary was the true heir. Another reason could possibly be that she were unlikely to produce a male heir so in theory there was no point including her, as her daughters would come next anyway. More importantly the younger the queen the more easily manipulated they could be, there was no way anyone would be able to rule through Frances.

The Scottish line descended from Margaret Tudor was also discounted which included her English born daughter Margaret Douglas but she was a devout catholic and never enjoyed a close relationship with Edward, she stayed away from court as much as possible on her northern estates where she was a practising catholic. She was also a very close ally of Marys which may have caused concern. The exclusion also meant that Mary, Queen of Scots whose claim out ranked Janes was also overlooked. So that leaves the protestant children of the Brandon sisters and the eldest was Lady Jane Grey. Jane and her sisters were first in line followed by Margaret Clifford, later Countess of Derby.

In theory then Lady Jane Grey was to be the heir to the throne of England but in order for Northumberland to rule through her, if indeed that was the plan, he still needed to find a way to control her. One thing Northumberland had was sons so he developed a plan to marry Jane to his younger son Guildford and through them he would wield power and in effect be nothing short of king. Jane had not been his first choice of bride for Guildford. In 1552 he approached the Earl of Cumberland for the hand of his daughter, Margaret Clifford (Eleanor Brandon's daughter) but the earl refused and asked the king to intervene. Edward declared that due to her father opposing the match, the wedding could not take place. Why Northumberland went for Margaret as the first option we do not know, maybe he felt she would bring Guildford more riches given her prominent role in the north of England. Or, maybe at that point Edward looked like he would marry and have children of his own meaning Jane and her sisters were not considered as important as they were in 1553. When his failure to bring Margaret Clifford into the fold with Guildford, he suggested a marriage between her and his brother, Sir Andrew Dudley. Again, this came to nothing but you can see Northumberland manoeuvring his pieces into place. He wanted his own people in positions of power and he knew the daughter of Eleanor Brandon was an important player in the game of Northumberland's domination.

In order to bring the marriage between Jane and Guildford to fruition the Suffolks needed to be party to the plan. Robert Wingfield explained Frances 'was vigorously opposed to it' but being a woman, she could not convince her husband, whose eyes were set on wealth and glory, to change his mind. At first Henry was not keen either on their prized eldest daughter marrying a younger son of a duke because it was not an equal match. Jane would not have been overly impressed at a match that seems quite a way beneath what she would have been expecting, but once again the promise of a crown appeared to change their minds and this time Jane was handed over to Northumberland. Either that or Suffolk was frightened of Northumberland and being the coward and wimp he was, he relented. The earliest mention of marriage talks between the two families came in April 1553 'The marriage was arranged by the duke not by chance but with a very precise purpose'. This statement gives us a clear indication that Northumberland was making plans but would anyone have thought for one second it was all part of a plan to put Jane on the throne? As far as people were aware, the king was ill but not too ill that the succession needed to be changed. The young couple were officially betrothed on 28 April, Frances was not overly keen on the idea because it usurped her good friend and cousin and she would have been well aware that if the plan failed it could mean serious repercussions for all those involved. Henry on the other hand never really thought about consequences and was happy to make any deal that gave his daughter a crown. Maybe he had hopes of ruling through Jane himself, was he planning to double cross Northumberland and sway Jane to his way of thinking? To be honest knowing what we do of Jane's strength of character I cannot imagine she would have let anyone rule for her, if she was to be queen then she alone would rule.

Frances's reluctance is interesting, many believe she was hard faced and stubborn but she never seems to be able to sway her husband away from his plans for their daughter. It also begs the question of how much did Frances actually know about the plan to place Jane on the throne at this time. It is hard to imagine Suffolk could have kept the details from her, if she knew something was being planned she would have forced the information out of him, he was too much a weak-willed man to be able to keep news like this to himself. Or, did the thought of Jane being queen regnant make her uncomfortable given she technically came before her in the order of succession, was Frances resentful that her daughter may get to wear the crown ahead of her? The likely reason is she seems to see the risk of Northumberland's plan but knew she was powerless to stop it because as a woman her thoughts would not be taken into consideration and regardless of her feelings, the king had approved of the union by giving it his blessing. Northumberland was going to get his match.

Of course, the independent and strong-willed Jane was not going to be happy with this news. Firstly, Guildford was just the fourth son, which to someone who had been told from birth they were destined for a great match must have been disconcerting and slightly worrying. In Tudor times children did not question their parents actions regarding their futures, girls especially were not to question the choice of husband but Jane was different. She was outspoken and obstinate and she voiced her concerns, much to her parents horror. She tried her best to resist the plans but eventually 'by the insistence of her mother, the threats of her Father' she had no choice but to submit to her parents orders. It is a commonly held belief that they beat Jane into submission. We can only speculate on that, but Jane was clearly forced into a marriage she did not want. But could this also be said of her groom, after all Guildford was in the same position. He was young and had this marriage forced upon him by his father in his unrelenting desire for power. Granted, it was a great match for him, he was marrying into the royal family and this no doubt was far beyond anything he could have ever wished for but who was Guildford Dudley? He was a younger son of John Dudley and his wife Jane Guildford, born in 1535 he was slightly older than Jane and like his future bride he was brought up in a protestant household with his siblings at the family seat Dudley Castle in the midlands. When in London the families resided at Ely Place. Unlike Jane's it was a loving family, his parents had married for love and had thirteen children together meaning he had plenty of playmates to romp around the grounds of Dudley Castle. Guildford was described by Richard Grafton as being 'comely, virtuous and goodly gentleman'. On paper he seems the perfect match for Jane, he comes across as a nice young protestant man who had been well educated. But would any man have ever matched up to Jane's high expectations? Maybe not.

There must have been many questions raised at court as to why someone who sits in line to inherit the throne would marry someone so far beneath her in status, if those questions were asked then Northumberland dealt with them. The wedding took place on 25 May in the chapel at Durham Place but the marriage of Jane and Guildford was not the only nuptials taking place that day. They were to share the day with Jane's younger sister Katharine, who was to marry Henry Herbert, the son and heir of the Earl of Pembroke, whilst Guildford's sister Katherine was married to Henry Hastings, the son and heir of the Earl of Huntingdon. Mary Grey was betrothed on the same day to Arthur Grey, Lord Grey de Wilton, but that wedding would not take place until she of an age to marry. It was a prosperous day for the Suffolk family, all three daughters were now either married or betrothed. On the face of it, assuming Jane knew nothing of the plan to put her on the throne, her younger sister appeared to be marrying better than the elder sibling, what reason was Jane given for this seemingly mis-matched marriage with Guildford? Her sister Katherine would one day be Countess of Pembroke and Katherine Dudley the Countess of Huntingdon but Guildford could bring Jane no title. Would the question not be raised as to why it was not Jane who was marrying into the Pembroke or Huntingdon family given their prominence? Yes Guildford is the son of a duke but on paper he brought Jane very little. It is commonly thought and accepted Jane was not aware of the plans to crown her queen, maybe her parents explained it away as being a good marriage that would seal an alliance with the powerful Dudley family, and seeing as Guildford was the eldest unmarried brother she was to marry him, no questions asked. But an intelligent girl like her would have smelt a rat she just perhaps could not figure out what the plan was. Jane would almost certainly not have known of King Edward's illness and would not question any potential loss of power for Northumberland.

As the wedding day dawned Jane would have woken with a feeling of dread in the pit of her stomach. She was not the excited blushing bride looking forward to marrying her true love, she was a young girl of 15/16 with a sense of foreboding over the coming days events. The king, who did not attend, had kindly paid for the clothes of all the wedding party. Jane was dressed in a luxurious gown of purple with silver and gold brocade which was encrusted in diamonds and pearls. Many influential guests gathered in the chapel at Durham Place to witness the three ceremonies take place. The vows were exchanged and the rings placed on fingers in front of the alter, before she knew it Jane was a married woman, albeit an unhappy and reluctant one. Forced to do her duty by her parents on what should have been a happy day was in fact a deeply unhappy one for her. Following the ceremonies, the guests moved to the great hall where a lavish banquet had been prepared. Jehan Scheyfve, ambassador to emperor Charles V, commented "On the 25th of this month were celebrated the weddings of my Lord Guilford, son of the Duke of Northumberland, to the eldest daughter of the Duke of Suffolk; of the Earl of Pembroke's son to the second daughter; and of the Earl of Huntingdon's son to the daughter of the Duke of Northumberland. The weddings were celebrated with great magnificence and feasting at the Duke of Northumberland's house in town."

Unfortunately, many guests, including Guildford, were struck down with food poisoning, which meant a reprieve for Jane as they were unable to consummate their union that night. Although it may have been pre-agreed that given their young age that duty could wait despite them both being an age to do so. Either that or Northumberland did not want to run the risk of Jane falling pregnant because the birth of a son would usurp her place from the succession. He may have also wanted a get out clause for Guildford should it be needed, there was every chance his plan could backfire spectacularly and he would need to distance himself as much as he could from Jane. So, following her wedding, Jane returned home with her parents to Charterhouse whilst her sister Katharine went to live with her new husband's family at Baynard's Castle which may indicate that marriage was consummated, but Katharine was only 12 years old so it is unlikely. Jane may have felt relief at not having to live with Guildford straight away but it did bring other issues. It meant the young couple could not get to know each other, and could not form a bond which would give them a good solid start to married life, but then this was a marriage that did not seem to take into consideration the feelings of husband or wife, it was the in-laws that mattered.

Jane was hoping the consummation would not happen for a while but those hopes were dashed when she was told it was time for her to leave her parents' home and move to Durham Place with her husband.

Chapter 8

'My Devise for the Succession'

In the February of 1553 Mary visited her ailing brother, during her time at court she was treated like the princess she rightfully was and there could have been no doubt at that stage she was the intended heir to the throne. There was no hint of a suggestion that Jane would be queen, or indeed anyone other than Mary would take the throne. Therefore, it must have been at some point between that visit to court and the writing of the first Devise four months later, that Edward decided to alter the succession. Now, whether Edward made that decision independently or whether someone (Northumberland) put the idea in his mind we do not know but history suggests it was not all Edward's idea.

At the beginning of June 1553 there were no legitimate male heirs of the royal house of Tudor, and there was no chance of one being born any time soon. King Edward VI lay dying in his bed at Greenwich and knew the time had come to consider who his heir should be so he drew up 'My Devise for the Succession'. This was a document that would change the line of succession to the English throne as previously stipulated in the will of his father King Henry VIII.

The pressure was building on Northumberland, he had to hope Edward would live until at least September when the new parliament convened in order to repeal the Act of Succession of 1544. It would make acceptance of the rewrite of the new Act much easier if the old one was no longer legally valid, So, in preparation Edward began to write down his own wishes for the future of the English monarchy. The first thing he did was remove his elder half-sisters the Ladies Mary and Elizabeth and seeing as both had been declared illegitimate by their father that was a fairly easy task, it was common knowledge they were illegitimate so the argument to remove them seemed sound.

Edward's Devise then goes on to state that a male heir of Frances, Duchess of Suffolk should inherit the throne. In the event she failed to produce a male heir (which was unlikely given her age and that she had not given birth for ten years) then the male heirs of Jane would inherit and so on through to Katharine and Mary Grey. If they did not produce any sons then the eldest daughter would inherit. It is clear at this stage that Edward did not fully understand how ill he was as he must have thought he had long enough to live to see either Frances or Jane conceive and give birth. But his illness progressed faster than anticipated and it soon became clear he was not going to live long enough to see either of them produce a male heir. So, he altered the Devise to read 'the Lady Jane **and** her male heirs' this change is crucial, any mention of Frances and her male heirs was removed and the line above inserted. The adding of that single word 'and' meant Jane herself was now able to claim the throne in her own right. It is remarkable to think that one minor word could alter the whole meaning of the document but it did and it set in motion one of England's most infamous periods of history.

How involved Northumberland was in the changing of the Devise we simply do not know. The traditional belief is that he put pressure on the ailing Edward to alter it to read in favour of Jane but Lucy Wooding suggests the Devise was all of Edwards making. As discussed earlier, Edward may have been a young king but he knew how to flex his kingly muscles and the writing of the Devise was his way of simply exercising his right to name his heir, just like his father had done before him. One thing was for certain, he would never agree to his sisters inheriting, Mary was catholic and Elizabeth was not popular due to her being the daughter of Anne Boleyn. In fact people saw her as illegitimate more than Mary because the people had a genuine love of Queen Katherine of Aragon and felt she was the true wife of Henry. What Edward ideally wanted was a strong male protestant leader but seeing as there was no male prince available, Jane represented the next best thing. Edward may have felt a certain affinity with her, they were of a similar age and had supposedly spent time together in the royal nursery but most importantly of all he knew she would uphold his reforms. Not only would Jane uphold all of Edwards reforms she would more than likely take them much further and that would appeal to many reformists. The king hoped committed protestants would support Jane because she had a reputation of being intelligent. She was respected for her intellect, well thought of and people like Archbishop Cranmer would support her, especially if it meant keeping Mary from the throne and to ardent reformists that was the ultimate aim.

But keeping Mary from the throne was not going to be easy, she knew it was her right by the will of her father so the decision was made to keep the Devise a secret. That may have seemed an easy thing to do, she did not reside at court so cutting her out of the loop so to speak was achievable but other members of the court knew something was going on. Northumberland knew that in order for the Devise to have any weight it would need to be legally ratified by parliament but they did not have the luxury of time, the king was on his death bed and urgent action was needed. Also, they could not just overturn Henry's will, that was a legally binding document so at the very least the Devise would have to be agreed upon by all of Edward's councillors. Each one signed their agreement on 21 June, some were reluctant but as they were bound to obey their sovereign in all things, they signed. Edward explained to those gathered that Mary and Elizabeth were his relations only by half-blood and that he had the right to pass his crown to whoever he saw fit. He also reminded them that his sisters were illegitimate and should they be allowed to take the crown they could marry a foreign prince who would expect to come and rule England as its king. On the plus side, Jane was already married, to an Englishman, making her the ideal successor.

Edward saw the Grey family as his true blood relations, they were his cousins and he even referred to them as his sisters. He considered them to have been brought up correctly and in the manner of his royal house and crucially they were of the right religion. It was a very persuasive argument and the reasons put forward by the king seemed perfectly logical and the speech had the desired effect. The Privy Councillors, the Archbishop of Canterbury, the Household officers and twenty-two peers of the realm signed the Devise and swore an oath that they would uphold it when the time came.

The Devise may have been signed and ratified by the most powerful men in the land but it left many of them with a feeling of unease and concern. In their minds Mary was the rightful heir as sealed in a legal binding document, this Devise was simply Edward's wish, that was to say it could not really change the order of succession in the eyes of the law. The Treason Act of 1547 made it an offence punishable by death to change the succession as stated in the 1544 Act of Succession, making what the men had done treason. This led to widespread panic about what would happen when Edward died. They knew Mary was not going to stand aside and watch her throne, which had been given to her by her father, be usurped. She had waited her whole life for this moment and had already shown her grit and determination to cling onto what was important to her. It wasn't just the fact that a different person would be sat on the throne that worried the council, it was the power struggle that would ensue over who was going to take real control because if by some miracle Jane did ascend the throne and manage to hang on to it then there was the issue of Northumberland and Suffolk. Both were power hungry and wanted to rule the country themselves, the councillors would have to bend to their will rather than Janes and that was definitely something they did not want to do. Having Mary as queen at least meant she would be capable of ruling independently.

But what of Jane? How much did she know of the plans to make her queen? History tells us she did not know at the stage the councillors signed the Devise. She had always been aware that she was important and had a place in the line of succession but that it was unlikely she would ever sit on the throne given Mary and Elizabeth came before her, so really it would be the last thing she was expecting. When she did find out from Northumberland that Edward was dying and that she had been named his heir she was utterly horrified, she

Lady Jane Grey. (WikiCommons)

Lady Katherine Grey.
(WikiCommons)

Lady Mary Grey.
(WikiCommons)

Guildford Dudley. (WikiCommons)

Edward Seymour, Lord Protector. (WikiCommons)

PARVVLE PATRISSA, PATRIÆ VIRTVTIS ET HÆRES
ESTO, NIHIL MAIVS MAXIMVS ORBIS HABET.
GNATVM VIX POSSVNT COELVM ET NATVRA DEDISSE,
HVIVS QVEM PATRIS, VICTVS HONORET HONOS.
ÆQVATO TANTVM, TANTI TV FACTA PARENTIS,
VOTA HOMINVM, VIX QVO PROGREDIANTVR, HABENT
VINCITO, VICISTI, QVOT REGES PRISCVS ADORAT
ORBIS, NEC TE QVI VINCERE POSSIT, ERIT.

Baby Prince Edward by
Hans Holbein the Younger.
(WikiCommons)

Above: King Edward VI.
(WikiCommons)

Right: Thomas Seymour.
(WikiCommons)

Katherine Parr. (WikiCommons)

John Dudley, Duke
of Northmberland.
(WikiCommons)

Mary Tudor and
Charles Brandon,
Duke and Duchess
of Suffolk.
(WikiCommons)

ANNO DNI   1 5 4 4

LADI MAR   DOVGHTER TO
THE MOST   VERTVOVS PRINC
KING HENRI   THE EIGHT

THE AGE OF   XXVIII YERES

Queen Mary I. (WikiCommons)

Young Lady Elizabeth. (WikiCommons)

My devise for the succession.

1. For lakke of issue of my body. To the L Fraces heires masles, to the L Janes heires masles, To the L Katerins heires masles, To the L Maries heires masles, To the heires masles of the daughters which she shal haue hereafter. Then to the L Margets heires masles. For lakke of such issue, To theires masles of the L Janes daughters To theires masles of the L Katerins daughters and so furth til you come to the L Margets daughters heires masles.

2. If after my death theire masle be entred into 18 yere old, then he to haue the hole rule and gouernance therof.

3. But if he be under 18, then his mother to be gouuernes til he entre is yere old. But to doe nothing without thaduise of 6 parcel of a counsel to be pointed by my last will to the nomore of 20.

4. If the mother die befor theire entre into 18 the realme to be gouuerned by the counsel. Prouided that after he be 14 yere al great matters of importaunce be opened to him.

5. If i died without issu, and ther were none heire masle, then the L Fraunces to be gouuernes. For lakke of her, the her eldest daughters and for lakke of them the L Marget to be

The Devise for the Succession. (WikiCommons)

Heinrich Bullinger by Hans Asper. (WikiCommons)

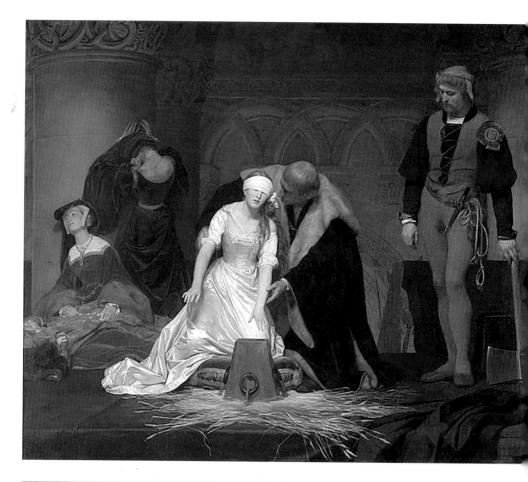

Above: The Execution of Lady Jane Grey by Paul Delaroche. (WikiCommons)

Left: Phillip II of Spain by Sofonisba Anguissola. (WikiCommons)

Charles Brandon,
Artist Unknown.
(WikiCommons)

The signature of Queen Jane. (WikiCommons)

Henry Brandon,
Duke of Suffolk
by Hans Holbein
the Younger, 1541.
(WikiCommons)

Charles Brandon,
miniature by Hans
Holbein the Younger,
1541. (WikiCommons)

King Henry VIII by Hans Holbein
the Younger. (WikiCommons)

John Aylmer,
Artist Unknown.
(WikiCommons)

ÆTATIS X
M·D·LX

Portrait thought to be that of Eleanor Brandon by Hans Eworth, it may also be a portrait of her daughter Margaret Clifford. (WikiCommons)

did not seek a crown, she did not want a crown and she certainly did not want the power and responsibility that came with a crown. Unfortunately for Jane her father and father-in-law did and she was to be the pawn that would get them that power. Knowing that her parents backed this outrageous plan must have left Jane feeling bereft of support and comfort. Having a daughter on the throne must have been a wonderful feeling for the Suffolks but the duke must have been aggrieved that Frances was being overlooked because if she became queen then he could become king. This very fact is more than likely the reason Henry VIII omitted Frances from his own order, the last thing he would have wanted was the realm being run by an incompetent fool. Having Henry Grey sat on the throne was also a situation Northumberland would not have wanted either, he could not wield power through the Suffolks which begs the question, was he behind Frances's omission from Edward's order of succession?

Despite her initial misgivings and the fact that she had also usurped her mother's place in the line of succession, Jane understood this to be god's will. Preventing Mary taking the throne and therefore preventing a return to Catholicism was of upmost importance to her. She felt she must take this burden on in order to save the people from that. Rumours that Northumberland had wanted the throne had been circulating the court for some time, he may have been an exemplary soldier but he was not well liked by the ministers, or the people. That however did not matter to him because he was feared which meant not many would have the strength or power to stand up to him, including the duke and duchess of Suffolk.

It was easier for them to hand Jane over rather than risk ostracization by Northumberland, she was like a lamb to the slaughter, the young innocent laid on the altar of sacrifice for the benefit of others. At least if the plan came off their daughter would be sat on the throne of England, whether they gave much thought to what would happen to her if the plan failed is questionable but their treatment of her when her reign of power came to an end tells us everything we need to know really, but more on that later. As a newly married woman Jane was desperate to return home but her mother-in-law, the influential duchess of Northumberland, refused her request and bade her to stay with her husband and his family. But the pressure of the situation made Jane ill so instead of returning to Sheen and her family she was granted permission to go to the former home of Katharine Parr in Chelsea. It had always been a happy place for Jane and here, in peace, she could remember the joyous times she had shared with her former mentor. It also put distance between her and the gossip filled streets of London. Guildford remained at Durham Place with his family and awaited further instruction.

Northumberland was continually working hard to secure support for the Devise, in order to allay any lingering doubts, he was supposedly offering bribes to councillors in an attempt to keep them onside. If any of them dared to defy him he would fight them, leaving them with little choice but to agree to his demands. They may have signed in support of their sovereign Edward in what was his dying wish but offering to support Northumberland was a whole different matter. It is interesting to ponder if the council would have wholeheartedly backed Jane as queen if she was ruling without Northumberland at her back, he never had the full loyalty of the council but that does not mean to say Jane would not. Northumberland's unpopularity and arrogance would be his ultimate downfall, and he would take Jane down with him.

The time was fast approaching when the plan would need to be put into action, Edward was getting weaker by the day and one of the most important aspects of the plan had not yet been finalised. In order for things to run smoothly Northumberland had to figure out some way of getting Mary and Elizabeth to Whitehall so he could apprehend them. The sisters were invited under the pretence they were coming to visit Edward to say their final goodbyes but he underestimated them both. Elizabeth suspected something was going on from the moment the invite came and declined the visit on the grounds that she was feeling unwell. Mary was a little more willing to believe the invitation was genuine and set off from her home at Hunsdon, north of London but at some point she decided to turn back, had she been given prior warning the invite was a trap? Maybe a member of the council had managed to make contact and get word to her what was happening. Either way she returned home and began to make plans of her own.

Northumberland was not aware of any of this, at this point he felt everything was under control and going to plan. The duke was not overly concerned by Elizabeth being a no show because he felt she could be easily apprehended without too much trouble. Mary was the main thorn in his side and she was about to fall into his trap, or so he thought. He must have gone to sleep soundly that evening believing his audacious plan was fool proof and thinking in a matter of weeks or even days his son would be sat on the throne of England as its king, with him pulling the strings behind the scenes. It wasn't just Jane he was aiming to dupe but his own son too. We are told his marriage and family life was happy with no scandal attached to any of the Dudley clan but is it a happy family that feels comfortable exploiting one another to get that bit ahead in life? What kind of father would be willing to put the lives of all his sons at risk for a crown? The Duke of Northumberland was that exact kind of father and he was too far mired in the plot now to do anything but continue down the road to utter annihilation.

Chapter 9

The Death of a King,
The Accession of a Queen

With his final words 'I am faint; Lord have mercy upon me, and take my spirit' King Edward VI of England died on 6 July 1553 at Greenwich Palace, he was just 15 years old and had reigned for over six years. As with many deaths at this time there were questions asked over the cause, many thought he had been poisoned by Northumberland and even though we cannot be certain, the cause of death was more than likely consumption. Northumberland had hoped to keep his death a secret for a further three days and away from the general public whilst he put the finishing touches to his plan. On the morning of the 7 July, he summoned the Mayor of London and the City Magistrates to Greenwich to advise them the king was dead and that they were to swear an oath of allegiance to Queen Jane, that news must have come as a shock. Jane was summoned from her refuge at Chelsea to the Tower of London where she was to claim her throne. Northumberland's daughter, Mary Sidney was tasked with escorting Jane from Chelsea to Syon House, the home of her father-in-law. They travelled up stream together by barge, Jane was in a deep state of shock and felt a huge sense of loss. Not only had she lost a cousin she held a respect and love for bringing her great sadness but she had also lost her old life. Gone were the days that she could spend lost in a book at Bradgate, her whole life had now changed with the death of the king.

As she disembarked her barge and walked up to the imposing house she found there was no one there to greet her. The new queen was made to wait for Northumberland and the council to arrive, was this planned?

Maybe Northumberland was sending Jane a clear message early on that he was the important one and she should be the one doing to waiting. Once the relevant people had assembled in the hall, including her father, they officially told Jane that Edward was dead and she was now queen. Once she had been proclaimed queen the gathered gentlemen knelt to pay homage to their new sovereign. Jane was mortified when they did and it caused her great embarrassment and unease. At some point after this, her mother, mother-in-law and the Marchioness of Northampton entered the room, Jane looked to her mother for support and reassurance but sadly she could provide her with neither, she was a queen now and therefore had to stand alone.

Much to her horror, Northumberland once again reiterated the news that Edward was dead and she had been named as his heir, as per his wishes. He read aloud the terms of the will; he informed Jane that should she remain childless her sisters would follow her. Following his speech, the gathered nobles knelt once more and swore their allegiance to her telling her they would defend her with their lives. Upon hearing this, the shell-shocked 16-year-old girl fell to the floor and wept at her misfortune. 'The crown is not my right and pleases me not. The Lady Mary is the rightful heir' she wailed as those gathered around her looked on in an uncomfortable silence. To imagine a girl so young thrust into such a situation is deeply concerning. How did they expect her to react? She was not the kind of girl who was going to leap for joy, run around the room shaking hands and thanking them for their support, if they thought she would then they clearly did not know Jane. This is another sign that Jane the person had not been given any thought, she was simply the vessel that carried the power, the royal blood that ran through the veins of the Grey sisters proved to be a curse for them all. Jane was a serious and sober young woman who would never take something that was not rightfully hers, unless she was force to do so. And forced she was.

But let us pause for a moment and reflect on what had actually happened in the great hall at Syon and question how much Jane actually knew about what was happening. Jane had been previously told by the

Duchess of Northumberland that she would be queen upon Edward's death. At that point she was horrified and knew she had no one in her immediate circle she could turn to. She had been isolated from her family but when she made the move to Chelsea was there no one in that household she could have reached out to? Anyone? All it would have needed was one loyal servant to carry a message to the right person, Mary even. Also, let us consider her relationship with Mary. We know she had a strong dislike for her. She had made personal attacks against her and her household and she had been rude and insolent towards her so would she not have relished getting one over on her catholic cousin? After all, Jane had been raised from birth to take on a great role and as one of the country's leading evangelical figures she would have seen this as god's will, and to Jane that was one thing she would never go against. The evidence would perhaps suggest this was not the case and that Jane had to be cajoled into taking the crown, her reaction at Syon is nothing short of utter horror but it is an interesting concept to think that just maybe she was not wholly innocent in this plot. That is not to say she went looking for the crown because I sincerely don't think she did, but when faced with the prospect of it, perhaps she could see what good she could do for the country and its people. She would not have been drawn to the crown for the riches and glamour, it would be the opportunity to carry on the reformist changes that would have lured Jane in.

By the time the nobles had pledged their allegiance, Guildford had arrived at Syon. Between him, Northumberland and her father the pressure on her to accept the crown was seemingly too much to withstand any longer. They knew that by telling her it was her religious duty to accept Edward's wishes she would relent. When this became about defending her religion she knew she had no choice but to go along with the plan, she had become a prisoner of other people's ambitions. They had trapped Jane in a religious snare, if she declined to do God's work then her very faith was blown to pieces and everything she stood for would be questioned. Those who admired her would question her beliefs and to Jane, what people thought of her in terms of religion mattered more than anything.

Over the next few days Jane remained at Syon, it was hoped she would come to terms with her new role before she was presented to her public. The public were in for a shock as they didn't even know their king was dead let alone the new monarch was not going to be who they thought it would. In the meantime, Northumberland threw a lavish and luxurious feast in Jane's honour at Syon, honouring her as their new queen. As Jane sat through the banquet she no doubt hated every second, battling in her head between was this God's true will for her or was she usurping the throne.

Four days after the death of Edward on the afternoon of 10 July Jane sailed from Syon downstream to the Tower of London, the impregnable fortress that she was now in control of. She made the journey accompanied by Guildford, her parents, mother-in-law and a select group of ladies of the court who would now be in attendance to the queen. Dressed in a sumptuous gown of green and gold with a long train that her mother bore, her headdress was white and jewel encrusted and the canopy of estate was carried over her head, signalling she was queen. Beside her was Guildford, dressed head to toe in white and gold, what was going through this young man's mind? They had not been wed long and it had not been a great start to married life and now he was escorting his wife and queen to the Tower to take up the reins of power. As Jane arrived at the royal stairs the heralds proclaimed her the new queen of England, unfortunately there was little enthusiasm for the news. There were no joyful voices shouting 'God save the Queen', instead, those gathered were stunned at the news, this was not the new queen they were expecting. It was a commonly held belief amongst the ordinary people of London that following Edward's death Mary would succeed, if not her then it would have been Elizabeth. King Henry had been incredibly popular during his early reign, he was young, good looking and intelligent and his people loved him, calling him 'Good King Hal'. Because of this, Mary and Elizabeth had been well loved too, Mary was especially well-liked due to the adoration of her mother queen Katherine. On the flip side of this, no one really knew who Jane was, she had never been a prominent figure at court and her parents were not overly popular so no one expected Henry's will to be challenged. It would appear the will had not just been challenged it had been torn up and completely disregarded. The mood amongst the crowd gathered at the Tower was not anger but more of shock and disbelief leaving them and the royal delegation at an awkward stand-off.

Jane and her entourage arrived at the Tower of London at 3pm in the afternoon and as she stood at the gates there was no great acclaim, cheers or good greetings which would have compounded her fears and reasserted her thoughts that this was wrong. She was nothing short of a usurper and everyone gathered there knew it. As she approached the doors to the Tower, Northumberland again fell to his knees and handed his queen the keys, he did his best to put on a show of royal grandeur but there was no escaping just how lacklustre it was, it was not the start to the reign they were hoping for. The death of King Edward VI was declared at 5pm and Jane was proclaimed Queen. As the proclamations were read across London and Mary declared a bastard daughter of the late king Henry VIII, it was announced that Edward VI had passed the crown to Jane. The Imperial Ambassador, Jehan Scheyfve described what happened as Jane arrived at the Tower:

> At about four o'clock this afternoon the ceremony of the state entry was performed at the Tower of London with the accustomed pomp. The new Queen's train was carried by her mother, the Duchess of Suffolk; and there were not many people present to witness the act. When it was over, criers at the street-corners published an order given under the Great Seal of England, by which, by the new Queen's authority, the Lady Mary was declared unfitted for the Crown, as also the Lady Elizabeth. Both ladies were declared to be bastards; and it was stated that the Lady Mary might marry a foreigner and thus stir up trouble in the kingdom and introduce a foreign government, and also that as she was of the old religion she might seek to introduce popery. However, no one present showed

any sign of rejoicing, and no one cried: "Long live the
Queen!" except the herald who made the proclamation
and a few archers who followed him. Thus your Majesty
may gather the state of feeling in England towards the
Lady Mary. We will endeavour to obtain a copy of the
above proclamation in order to send it to your Majesty.

The city's inhabitants looked on in dismay and confusion, this
was not acceptable. The irony was that it was not acceptable for
Jane either, the only people who truly thought she was queen were
Northumberland and her father.

No one at the Tower dared speak out against Jane's rise to the
throne but the general public in London were a different matter. One
man was punished for speaking out against Jane. Gilbert Potter had
his ears cut off for daring to challenge the accession of Jane, many
agreed with him but did not dare speak out in public for fear of
punishment. Because the people were too scared to raise their voices
against the new monarch on the face of it looked like the people
backed Queen Jane. The councillors seemed to have accepted her and
the public seemed content, they were not jubilant at the news but at
the same time there was no show of anger or rebellion towards their
new queen. Northumberland had done his job in subduing the people
and he had miraculously proclaimed Jane Queen.

Once inside the Tower Jane was taken to the royal apartments
where she tried to come to terms with just how disastrous her arrival
had been. If she was hoping to feel reassured by the public she was
greatly let down. The lack of enthusiasm must have been a cause
for concern for everyone but the queen did not have long to think
about her troubles before she was called to the presence chamber to
greet her councillors. She entered the chamber where she sat upon
her throne under a canopy of state and there was no escaping the fact
that she was their queen. They were seeing it with their own eyes, to
all intents and purposes Northumberland had succeed in putting his
daughter-in-law Lady Jane Grey on the throne of England.

Phase one of the plan was a success but what of his son Guildford, where exactly did he fit in his father's plans? If it had been Northumberland's and indeed Guildford's plan to crown him king, Queen Jane had other ideas. When she was handed the crown jewels by the Lord Treasurer, William Paulet, Marquess of Winchester she baulked at the idea of wearing the crown, he offered to place it on her head, as was her right as queen. She did her best to resist him but after he had reassured her again that it was her right as queen, she relented. Queen Jane took the crown from him and placed it on her head, this was a pivotal moment in Jane's story as queen. How did she, the most ardent of reformists and shunner of all things showy and grand feel when she placed the most ornate item of the crown jewels upon her head? Was she exhilarated or horrified that it had come to this. As she sat upon her throne wearing the crown it must have been then that she truly accepted her fate and her duty as Queen of England. She could not have known it at the time but the acceptance of the crown would be an action that would be used in the case against her, used to prove she was complicit in the whole plot.

The Marquess then turned to Jane and commented that a crown ought to be made for Guildford, it had never crossed her mind until that point that Guildford would expect to be crowned king alongside her but as far as she was concerned Edward left the crown to her, not them jointly. Had that whole scenario been orchestrated to raise the issue of Guildford becoming King? It may well have been but all it did was make Jane see what was really happening, the clouds parted and she finally saw clearly what Northumberland was up to, he wanted his son crowned so he could rule through him. She absolutely refused to agree to him being king, the best she would offer was a dukedom, maybe the dukedom of Clarence would suit Guildford. Jane was playing Northumberland at his own game, he thought he could manipulate her into doing as he wished, but Jane was much more resolute than he gave her credit for. Of course, Guildford and his father were not going to be satisfied with a dukedom, the last Duke of Clarence had been the ill-fated George Plantagenet brother of Edward IV, he was executed on his brother's orders apparently choosing to drown him in a butt of malmsey wine, was there any significance in Jane choosing that particular dukedom to offer to her husband? Was it a warning to him and his father that she was queen and she alone would decide on matters of state.

This was a blow for Guildford as he had more than likely been lured into this marriage by his father with the promise of a crown, now it seemed that was to be taken from him so he turned to his mother. The duchess of Northumberland advised her son to stop visiting Jane's bed until she relented, thinking that would be a punishment to her of course that was probably a welcome break for Jane. When that failed to move Jane, he went on to threaten to leave the Tower altogether and leave Jane to face her queenship alone but again she was unmoved. Jane was stubborn and was not willing to be her husband's puppet, she ordered him to stay at the Tower and refused to bend to his will and again refused point blank that he would ever be crowned alongside her. Guildford stayed although in a few days' time he probably wished he hadn't. Jane reiterated that if they wanted her to be queen then they had her alone, she would rule as Queen regnant or not at all, making her the first the country had ever had.

The news of Edward's death and Jane's accession had to be circulated and fast. Letters were sent to magistrates the length and breadth of the country requesting they spread the news amongst their towns and villages that the king was dead and to swear allegiance to the new queen, Jane. But there was still the issue of Mary. Everyone knew she would not slip away quietly but at this early stage it truly looked like Jane held all the power and they were in a strong position, which they probably were given they had control of the Tower but Mary was amongst her own people plotting her next move. Queen Jane had dealt with her husband and in-laws, but now she had to deal with the woman whose throne, many believed, she had stolen. The only way she could ever feel safe and secure on that throne was to act fast. The problem for Jane and Northumberland was the Lady Mary was just as stubborn and strong-willed; only one queen could sit on the throne and the time had come to finally settle who that would be.

Chapter 10

Jane, the Queen

The Lady Mary had always been popular with the people of England and was regarded as Henry VIII's legitimate daughter and so it seemed natural she would succeed Edward as queen. Since the king's death no one knew the exact whereabouts of Mary but before long a messenger arrived at the Tower of London. Thomas Hungate arrived to tell Queen Jane and her councillors that Mary was aware of her brother's death and that Jane had been proclaimed queen. She demanded Jane be renounced immediately and that the councillors recognise her as their true queen. She kept her tone calm and measured and offered the hand of friendship by advising she was willing to offer pardons to those members of the council who had been forced into supporting Jane. It must have been common knowledge that Northumberland had been offering bribes to get the councillors onside.

Naturally Northumberland was not happy at this request and threw the elderly Hungate into a dungeon telling him he should have had more sense given his age. The reply sent to Mary stated that Jane had been invested and proclaimed queen as per the wishes of King Edward VI in his letters patent, they also reminded her that she had been proclaimed illegitimate by her own father and so she would be better to submit to Jane and be obedient. But Mary was not one for submitting and accepting a situation if she felt it was wrong, she held out against her father for a long time and refused to accept her parents' divorce, and against Edward refusing to renounce her faith. It seems incredulous to believe that Northumberland felt she would accept Jane as queen, he knew first-hand how obstinate she could be but with Mary making contact the next phase of the plan could commence. Until now Mary had been out of sight, out of mind but now she had made a move and her feelings known, the councillors had to decide whether to carry on supporting Jane or switch allegiance to Mary. But before they could do that, they needed to know where Mary was based.

Mary had known something was wrong before Edward died, she knew there was some kind of plot to stop her ascending the throne. She also knew she had to get to safety, and quickly. On the day the king died she decided to flee Hunsdon and head into East Anglia. She knew she would have support there so she went straight to her home at Kenninghall, north-east of Bury St. Edmunds, from there she would have been able to gain a much bigger support base. It was whilst at Kenninghall she was told the king, her brother, had died and that Jane had been proclaimed queen. She knew there was a plot but would she for one second have thought it would be her cousin's daughter Jane Grey that would attempt to oust her from her throne? Shocked at this news Mary was defiant. She was going to fight for her throne as that was her birth right, she was the daughter of a king, unlike Jane Grey. To Mary the fact her father had stressed in his will that she would succeed Edward should he not have any legitimate heirs meant everything to her and it was that fact she based her bid for the throne.

It was from Kenninghall she sent Hungate with his message, it was important that Northumberland, and Jane, knew she was going to fight and not just stand aside whilst her throne was usurped. The council had to play the game very carefully too, not only did Mary have support in England but she could turn to her cousin and the Holy Roman Empire for support. The emperor Charles V had long voiced his support for Mary which had England on tenterhooks for much of Edward's reign due to the pressure they placed on Mary to convert to Protestantism. But for now, whilst they were on alert and ready to come to Mary's aid if needed, their initial reaction was to reply to Mary and reiterate that Jane was queen on the basis that Mary was illegitimate and Edward had wished the crown to go to

Jane. Basically, they expected Mary to just accept this and move on, how they underestimated her, and her supporters. By the 12 July she had moved on to Framlingham Castle in Suffolk. It was considered to be the most secure and safest castle in the area, and as Mary had anticipated, East Anglia was coming out for her. Most crucially the city of Norwich declared for her and sent her armed troops and that provoked an avalanche of support across the region as they were soon joined by many more from across the area, men who were there to defend her right to rule, regardless of religion.

Robert Dudley was sent into East Anglia in an attempt to secure Mary's person, he had already missed his opportunity earlier when she was staying at Hunsdon but by now she was well protected. His other task was to raise support for Jane, his sister-in-law, which he did well. He managed to secure King's Lynn in support of Jane, which at the time was Norfolk's second city so was seen as quite a coup. He also had to ensure the country was well defended should the emperor follow through with his threat to attack. One of the measures put in place was to position ships from the royal fleet off the coast of Yarmouth in the North Sea. From here they could keep watch on any enemy ships attempting to get close to rescue Mary, descend on London or cause all-out rebellion.

The Duke of Suffolk was requested to lead Jane's army into East Anglia but he was not the born leader Northumberland was and based on his previous reluctance to fight he blustered and suggested Northumberland took on the task instead. There was no denying Northumberland was the country's foremost soldier so it would seem like the obvious choice. Jane had wanted her father to go and defend her right to the crown but once again Frances stepped in with the clear thinking, she was conscious this plan may well falter and if it did they would want to survive. If Mary became queen it would look much better if Suffolk was not leading the army that had been sent to capture her. He was also suffering from ill-health; he was experiencing bouts of fainting alongside painful stomach complaints which had more than likely been brought on by the stress and anxiety over the previous few days. Instead, it was decided he would stay in London to defend his daughter in the Tower and be close by to offer support in a more political way. Again, he did not have much political acumen, it is hard to know which position Henry Grey would cause the least amount of trouble for Jane, in the army on the battlefield or at the council table because he had a proven track record of being a liability at both. There is no doubt though that Jane would have felt more comfortable with her father by her side.

As much as it grated on him, Northumberland knew he had no choice but to lead from the front. It may have been the right choice in terms of military experience but he was reluctant to leave London because he felt his place was to be near the power at the Tower. This was his plan and he was needed to control events there, not on a dusty road somewhere between London and East Anglia. There was also the worry that Suffolk was not a strong enough leader to keep the council together. For Jane though having her father close by gave her a sense of reassurance and she knew he would be loyal to her unto the last. Unfortunately, Northumberland was right, before he had even left London news filtered through that more and more people were flocking towards Mary, he had to move fast in assembling his troops together. It was imperative they nipped any possible rebellion in the bud, and if Jane was to remain secure on the throne Mary had to be dealt with. The council struggled to raise the great numbers of men they had hoped for, they were short on man and horse power and had very little artillery available to them. Before leaving, Northumberland had to ensure London was well protected in his absence, he ensured the guns at the Tower were mounted and ready to fire should the need arise. He mustered his men at Durham Place, his army consisted of 2000 men on horseback and 3000 soldiers on foot, it was suggested he had to pay over inflated wages including a month's pay upfront just to enlist these men although there is no evidence to support this. He had approximately twenty pieces of artillery at his disposal.

They left on the morning of 14 July in confident mood knowing they had at their back all the royal armoury had to offer, he assumed he had plenty in back up should it be needed. As the royal army moved through the streets of London they were met with an uneasy silence. The country stood on the brink of civil war and the people wholly blamed Northumberland for that. Sir John Gates left London later that afternoon at the head of the Household Cavalry. He took with him the artillery with essential supplies following the day after. On the face of it this should be a swift and easy victory for the royal forces, but little did they realise just how popular Mary was in East Anglia.

The royal forces managed to travel twenty-five miles on the first day and made it as far as Ware, Hertfordshire, where more troops joined the ranks and where Northumberland was joined by his sons. The following morning, they set off heading for Cambridge and from there they would set their sights on Framlingham and Mary. But Northumberland's initial concerns seemed to be coming true because as soon as he left London the lords started to defect to Mary. It seems they were just waiting for the first opportunity to turn their backs on Jane and her cause and Suffolk clearly had no authority over them to keep them onside. He had never been a well-respected man and was largely ineffective when it came to negotiating, persuading and bending people to his will. He had no persona like Northumberland, he did not strike fear into any man so he had no choice but to resort to desperate measures. The only option available to Suffolk was to order the gates of the Tower to be locked so that no one could leave, and if they tried, he would know about it. It all smacks of desperation, they knew Jane's hold on the crown was slipping pretty much from day one and this was all they could do to keep everyone together. These kinds of tactics only serve for so long, people get restless and resentment grows but by keeping them all together also provides the rebel councillors with an opportunity to plot.

In an attempt to dazzle the councillors and project Jane's majesty she was offered the crown jewels again. It was important that she looked like a queen and behaved with authority, how could they be expected to rally to her cause if she looked like a meek 16-year-old girl? In her regalia as queen, Jane would have looked majestic, authoritative and regal, it would have given the men something to cling to because their queen was visable to them, she was among them and not in a castle in Suffolk planning a rebellion.

But whilst Queen Jane sat in the Tower in her finery, Mary was at Framlingham seeing more and more men flock to her cause and when the news came that the royal fleet had abandoned Jane and turned for her she was delighted. This was a pivotal moment; it was a huge blow for Northumberland who now saw the south west coast of England undefended and open to attack, if the emperor did decide to send troops there would have been an open door and the country would have been flooded with foreign troops. But it was not all bad news for Jane, on the 16 July Nicholas Ridley, Bishop of London preached at St Paul's Cross reminding people that Mary and Elizabeth were illegitimate by the admission of their own father and that Jane was the rightful queen and people should accept her as so. The response to this message was met with an uneasy silence, the people had clearly not accepted their new monarch. Also, on that day a note was left at St Paul's supporting Mary's claim and then on the eighteenth a poster was put up claiming the rest of the country had risen in support of Mary as the true queen and London should follow suit. London may have been the capital, the heart of government and the crown but the rest of the country still mattered. What the council did not want was London becoming isolated in its ideas, you could not have a queen of London and a queen of the rest of the country so London had to decide whose banner it was going back.

Parliament had already begun to work in Queen Jane's name and she began signing her letters Jane, The Queen, she had clearly accepted her fate, whether she was glad about it or not she accepted this was her lot in life now so she had better get on with it. More men flocked to Mary's rally cry and her numbers were only expected to grow. Northumberland needed to get to Mary as soon as possible before he was outnumbered and outmanoeuvred, he managed to reach

Bury St Edmunds by the 17 July, he was stationed just twenty-four miles from Framlingham and when news reached him that Mary's numbers were swelling he requested back-up from the council but it was not forthcoming, was this a sign they had deserted or had the message just not got through?

The ever steady and confident Duke of Northumberland began to panic and decided to retreat back to Cambridge. He knew he needed more men and must have hoped to have been able to recruit them from there and the surrounding areas. He had expected more troops to join at Newmarket but they were not forthcoming, the signs were starting to show that all was not going to plan. He must have known by now the council had started to desert Jane and turned over to Mary by the lack of support that came from the capital. He would also have recognised that once a small group had deflected it was only a matter of time before they all turned their coats. But it wasn't just men from East Anglia that were joining Mary, in the ultimate blow, Northumberland's own troops now began to desert him. Once this happened he must have known the cause was completely lost, Jane's reign was no longer tenable, she could hold onto the crown no longer and he had failed to keep her on the throne with not one weapon raised in anger. Mary had won simply because the people recognised her as the true and rightful queen.

When the time came for Northumberland to march his troops on Mary he seems to have made strange choices in regards to the route taken. He chose to go via Cambridge and Bury St Edmunds, a journey of over 115 miles when a much shorter route was open to them. If he had decided to go via Colchester and Ipswich then he could have brought the distance to under 100 miles. With the urgency required why did he do this? You would have expected him to take the most direct route but actually what he was doing was backing Mary into a corner. With the sea behind her and with no easy access out of East Anglia, she had very few options available to her. If he had chosen to go via Colchester he may have spooked her and forced her to flee the country using one of the many ports along the east

Anglian coast. Northumberland would have assumed the royal fleet could have intercepted her had she decided to leave but they had turned in her favour by now anyway. This was a battle that the great soldier Northumberland should never have lost. He had Mary in a tight grip when he was at Bury St Edmunds, that was his time to advance, but he retreated instead. Despite the news of people joining her cause he still had the power to seize her at that point.

The retreat back to Cambridge seems a strange move considering he was just twenty miles from Framlingham; Eric Ives suggests this could be down to a lack of provisions and the no show of the reinforcements but in reality it was probably the fact that Mary's forces were growing so fast that they were simply outmanoeuvred. Mary also instilled a sense of righteousness in her followers and when the Earl of Sussex came over to her side it made it all the more difficult for Northumberland. Ives goes on to suggest what he perhaps should have done was to proceed to Framlingham and force Mary's supporters into combat, many of them were not seasoned fighters, surely it would have been best to force the fight than back away completely. Just what did he think was going to happen to him if he retreated? He knew he would have been captured and more than likely executed so why not die in a blaze of glory in battle fighting for a cause that he himself started. He had heard the rumours that Mary had artillery at Framlingham and he was not willing to engage in that kind of war, so he retreated. Maybe he was thinking of those men that were still under his command, not wanting to send them to almost certain death. But the question remained as to where the artillery had come from, the only artillery in the country should be based at the Tower of London, and that was at Northumberland's disposal. Northumberland must have been flabbergasted to discover it had come from the boats docked out at sea. When he learnt they had deserted him his heart must have sunk, at that point he knew there was no chance of winning, it was the most pivotal moment of the rebellion. It has been suggested that was the news he received in Bury St Edmunds which left him no option but to retreat.

There are many holes to pick at regarding Northumberland's failure. Had he not dithered when leaving London then things might have turned out differently for him and Jane but it was too late now. The attempt to put Jane on the throne and keep her there had ended in failure. Of course, it was not all down to the duke there were things beyond Northumberland's control that he could never have anticipated. For one, the will of the people, he had clearly underestimated their love of Mary. The turning of his fleet and troops so quickly and the lack of ability Suffolk had in keeping the council together. It would seem they had been fighting a losing battle from the start.

Back at the Tower, the fractured council, Jane and her parents patiently waited for news but they knew what was coming, defeat. Slowly, one by one the councillors left the Tower and pledged their allegiance to Mary. By the 18 July, Jane sat in the Tower with just her parents, Guildford, his mother and a handful of ladies for support. It must have made for a desperate and pitiful sight, to see a young 16-year-old girl frightened at what the future held for her. All her supporters had quickly realised she was a lost cause and did everything they could to distance themselves from her. The main supporter she lost was the Earl of Pembroke, his son had married Jane's younger sister Katharine needless to say that marriage was quickly annulled and the unfortunate girl sent back to her family in ruin.

The councillors headed straight for Pembroke's home at Baynard's Castle to pledge allegiance to Mary. The next step was to inform the Mayor of London and Aldermen who then joined the Privy Council at Baynard's Castle where the Earl of Pembroke publicly proclaimed Mary Queen of England, much to the delight of those gathered. A *Te Deum* was read at St Paul's in celebration. The proclamation of Mary was like a huge weight being lifted of the shoulders of London, relieved there had been no bloodshed and happy to have their true and rightful queen on the throne.

It was all over. Northumberland proclaimed Mary queen on 20 July. The people were celebrating on the streets of London, their beloved Lady Mary was now Queen Mary and Jane was all but forgotten. The Council came to the Tower to confirm Suffolk's worst fears, his daughter had been ousted and she was no longer queen. After hearing this news, he went to Jane in the royal apartments and tore down the canopy of state which was held over her head whilst she was dining with Guildford. He told her 'this place did no longer belong to her' and that 'she must put off your royal robes and be content with a private life' which was wishful thinking on his part. Upon hearing her father's words Jane must have felt a surge of relief course through her, her nightmare was over. She had never wanted the crown and was more than happy to pass it back to the rightful heir but if she thought she was going to be able to return to her former life she was sadly mistaken, she knew there had to be some form of punishment. At the insistence of others, she had usurped the throne and she must have known she was not going to escape that without some kind of retribution. The tables had turn and she was now at Mary's mercy. How her cousin would treat her was unknown she just had to sit in the Tower and wait hoping Mary did not bear grudges. In a flash Jane had gone from being the queen of England who gave the orders to powerful men to just a young girl who obeyed them, Jane and Guildford were now prisoners.

Whilst Jane sat and waited, the Earl of Arundel and Sir William Paget rode to Framlingham to advise Mary that Jane was no longer queen and that she had finally been proclaimed queen. As they handed her the great seal of England, they told her how the bells of St Paul's rung out in glee. Mary must have felt elated and relieved, without an ounce of blood spilt she had conquered and she could now ride to London in glory.

All the while Mary and her supporters celebrated poor Jane found herself alone. In an act of utter abandonment her parents fled the Tower in the hope they could receive a pardon from Mary. Without a care for their daughter, they went to pledge their allegiance to Mary hoping it would be enough to save their heads. Suffolk went to Tower Hill to publicly proclaim Mary as queen, from there he then went home to Sheen to join the rest of his family, they had to hope Frances's good relationship with Mary would help them.

Jane's ladies all left her, one by one they walked out of the Tower and back to their lives. In the end everyone deserted Jane apart from Guildford, he remained at her side to take his punishment with her. His mother, the Duchess of Northumberland had been ordered to remain at the Tower, she had been remanded there to await her own fate when her husband returned. As nightfall came the agonising wait was over, the guards had come to escort them to their prisons. Guildford was lodged in the Beauchamp Tower and Jane was housed in the home of Nathaniel Partridge, Gaoler of the Tower of London. They were ordered to stay there until further orders were given. It must have been terrifying for Jane; she was having to face punishment alone for an act she had no say in. Did she feel angry, upset, indifferent? All we can be grateful for is that she had her God to comfort and guide her through the next few agonising hours.

As his son and daughter-in-law and his wife were imprisoned in the Tower, Northumberland was still at large and needed to be apprehended. Queen Mary handed this responsibility to the Earl of Arundel as an opportunity to prove his loyalty to her. He was tasked with tracking Northumberland and his supporters down and word soon got back to him that he was lodged at the house of John Cheke in Cambridge. Arundel and his men came hammering on the door and arrested the duke whilst in his bed. He begged to be treated leniently claiming he had only acted as the council had instructed him to do so. Arundel was unmoved by his former friends pleas and remained loyal to Mary and took Northumberland and three of his sons John, Ambrose and Henry and his brother Sir Andrew Dudley, into custody, the Lord Robert Dudley would follow closely behind.

It was an uncomfortable journey back to London for the Dudley men. En route they were pelted with stones and dirt, obscenities were shouted at them by the public who let them know in no uncertain terms they were despised and deserved the punishment that was coming their way. When the party arrived at the Tower of London they were greeted by Constable Sir John Gage and the Lieutenant Sir John Brydges. The duke was lodged in St Thomas's Tower whilst the brothers joined Guildford in the Beauchamp Tower which would have brought some comfort to him.

The Dudley men's fate seemed pretty certain but for others it was a twitchy time. Those men who had initially backed Jane, especially those that signed the Devise were in for a worrying time. Whilst Mary was grateful for their support in the end they would have to face some kind of punishment in return for their pardon. They would probably face a monetary donation to the royal coffers which in all fairness is a pretty lenient sentence but Mary knew she would need a council and those men were just the men she needed.

Queen Mary, dressed in regal purple and gold velvet made her triumphant state entrance into London on the evening of 3 August, her half-sister Lady Elizabeth was by her side with a show of Tudor solidarity. She arrived at the gates of the Tower of London around 7pm, no doubt Jane could hear the applause as she arrived whilst she sat in her prison. Knowing Mary was in residence must have been a great cause of anxiety and all Jane could do now was hope the queen would show her some leniency. One of the first things Mary did was order the release of all catholic prisoners from the Tower, including the aging Duke of Norfolk and Bishop Stephen Gardiner. Another to benefit from Mary's goodwill was her cousin Edward Courtenay who she created Earl of Devon and Knight of the Bath. He had been incarcerated in the Tower for fifteen years following his parents arrest for leading a potential catholic uprising with the support Cardinal Reginald Pole. Courtenay's mother was a close friend of the queen and she secured his release, this would have been encouraging for Jane as it shows Mary dealt favourably with those close to her. Family connections were important to Mary so Jane had reason to believe she too would be looked upon favourably. Although if that was to happen she would have to desist in her attacks on the queens religion, she condemned Catholics and those who were attending mass, including Mary. At times her language is acerbic and venomous and it did her cause no good. It begs the question if Jane realised at all how much danger she was in, was her judgement clouded by her absolute zealous attitude to religion.

It had been just thirteen days since King Edward had died but within that time England was already on its second queen. Jane had technically been queen for the full thirteen days but had reigned for just nine of those days. She had been nothing but a puppet for men with grand ideas of power, she had been married against her will, had an unwanted crown thrust upon her head and now she had to sit and wait to find out what punishment she would receive for other people's ambitions. It is hard not to feel sadness for this young girl who through no fault of her own got caught up in a ridiculous plot to make her queen.

Chapter 11

Mary Triumphs

Queen Mary's journey back to London from Suffolk was one of joy and delight, she was cheered through every town and broke her journey at one of her favourite homes, Beaulieu. It was here that Mary and Frances came face to face when, in the early hours of 30 July Frances arrived and requested an audience with the queen. Mary must have been expecting this moment, maybe even dreading it given the closeness of the two cousins. She granted Frances her request which gave her the opportunity to plead forgiveness for her family. She started with her husband, predictably she blamed everything on Northumberland stating it was all his idea, he did all the planning and made it impossible for him to decline. She even went as far as accusing the duke of poisoning her husband in a bid to weaken him, or maybe even kill him so Jane had no male protector. There could be a small amount of truth to this claim given Suffolk had been struck down with severe stomach complaints that left him bed ridden at times, the pains were that bad Frances feared he would die from his illness.

Mary was sympathetic to a point; she agreed to release Suffolk from the Tower and instead placed him under house arrest at Sheen but he was to be warned that one step out of line and he would be returned back to the Tower and there would be no second chance. He was released the day after Frances's request was granted and he skulked back to Sheen and the family kept their heads down and out of trouble. The marriage between Lady Katherine Grey and Lord Herbert was annulled which left them heartbroken as they had grown close and there was a genuine affection between the young couple. In their desperation to stay together they went as far as stating the marriage had been consummated but given Katherine was only 13 years old it was unlikely it had. Young Mary's betrothal had also been broken and both girls returned home, shamed by their sisters actions they were just another casualty of the whole tragic situation. Did they know the full extent of what had happened? Katherine probably understood fully what had been happening but Mary was maybe just a bit too young to fully grasp the dire situation the family had been placed. Did they realise their elder sister had been pushed into taking the crown or did they assume she had taken it willingly and she was a true traitor? If they knew their sister well they would have known none of this was any of her doing, but whether they knew how involved their parents had been in forcing the crown on their sisters head we do not know. Sadly, their feelings from the time are not recorded, they were children and female children at that so no one would have given them a second thought.

But what of her daughter? Sadly, there is no record that Frances spoke on behalf of Jane which sounds incredibly uncaring and harsh but there may well be an element of not wanting to push her luck with Mary. She could not risk her changing her mind regarding her husband, she needed him at home with their two younger daughters, Jane would have to wait. It seems incredibly harsh (yet probably true) but Ives suggests Frances simply 'wrote off' her daughter; self-preservation was key and if that meant abandoning your daughter to face her fate alone to save your family, then so be it. The two cousins were close and perhaps Frances thought there was no chance Mary would punish Jane when she heard how little she had to do with the plot. However, from Mary's point of view, she was presented with documents Jane signed as the queen and she authorised the raising of an army against her which is pretty compelling evidence. As Frances left Beaulieu to be reunited with her husband at Sheen she had to hope Mary's good nature stretched to her daughter as the alternative did not bear thinking about. Jane continued to languish in the Tower with no apparent support coming her way.

It was an act of mercy Mary had shown the Suffolks, but they were family and that mattered but she was in no mood to be as kind when the Duchess of Northumberland came knocking at her door for an audience. She had been released from the tower once her husband and sons were safely ensconced behind the fortresses walls and her first task was to head to the queen and plead on their behalf for leniency. Once Mary had heard she was approaching she sent word that it would be best to turn back and return to London, the queen was refusing to see her. It was clear to see who Mary was blaming for the usurpation of her throne, it was felt maybe Jane would be freed in time and the Dudley family would take the full brunt on her anger.

As Jane sat in her rooms at the Tower she must have been eager to get her side of the story across to Mary but she knew she would not be allowed access to her, so instead she decided to write down her full account of the events that unfolded over those thirteen days. There is no evidence to back this up but we can be fairly sure this account reached the queen given her belief that Jane was innocent of all wrong doing. She fully accepted that Jane had been coerced and bullied into doing what she did. That said, there was to be no release and Jane was to remain in the Tower. Jane's life looked to be safe but Mary still needed to decide on the best way to deal with her. In an interview with Jean Scheyfve, the Imperial Ambassador, Mary indicated no pardons had been issued to any of those who had been complicit in the plot but that Jane was different, she was struggling with her conscience and at that point had no intention of sending her young cousin to the block. Jane had to be patient but it looked like in time she would gain her freedom.

Northumberland on the other hand was a different matter, his trial was set for 18 August and was held at Westminster Hall. He was tried alongside his eldest son John, Earl of Warwick and Thomas Parr, Marquess of Northampton, the brother of Queen Katharine Parr. He was to be tried by his peers which was ironic considering many of them had been his supporters just matter of weeks earlier. The elderly Thomas Howard, Duke of Norfolk presided over the trial in his role as Lord High Steward. He himself had only just been released from the Tower of London by Mary after being imprisoned since 1546 following his admittance of treason in covering for his son. The Earl of Surrey had added the arms of King Edward the Confessor to his own personal coat of arms. Surrey was executed and Norfolk was found guilty and condemned to die on 28 January 1547, saved only by the death of Henry VIII that same morning.

As the trial began Northumberland told those gathered that he had only acted on the wishes of his sovereign King Edward VI and his councillors and that he was being made a scapegoat, whilst everyone else walked free. It was clear he was going to be the one to suffer. He pleaded on his knees to be pardoned, asking the queen to show his five sons mercy but his pleas fell on deaf ears and he was found guilty of high treason and condemned to die a traitors death. The Earl of Warwick, who pleaded guilty to all the charges, and the Marquess of Northampton were also found guilty and condemned to the same fate. Northumberland had to face the agony of knowing his son and heir was going to lose his head. He begged 'that her Majesty may be gracious to my children ... considering they went by my commandment who am their father, and not of their own free wills'.

The three condemned men were sent back to the Tower to await their terrible fates. Northumberland did not have long to wait; his execution was initially planned for 8am on 21 August but at the last minute he decided to abandon his protestant faith and return back to his catholic roots and thereby cancelling the execution for that day. Knowing Queen Mary was a devout catholic he did this in the hope it would appeal to her kind nature, he made a request of being allowed to hear mass one last time. His request was granted and the execution was pushed back to the following morning. He attended mass at St Peter ad Vincula where he took communion and made public his wish to return to Catholicism, the Earl of Warwick did the same the day after, except Northumberland was told he was to die the next morning and Warwick was returned to his cell. That evening before his death, Northumberland knew 'that I must prepare myself against tomorrow to receive my deadly stroke'

On the morning of 22 August 1553, the Duke of Northumberland was led from his cell in the Tower of London to his place of execution. In front on nearly 10,000 spectators, he stood on the scaffold and admitted his guilt he then said his prayers and led his head on the block. The executioner removed his head with one blow of the axe. When he lifted the severed head he held it up to the huge crowds and they cheered, the hated Duke of Northumberland was dead! The Marquess of Northampton was spared death and released from the Tower months later, he converted back to Catholicism which seems to have been his saving grace. To Jane, the deserting of the protestant faith in a bid for freedom was the biggest crime these men could ever commit, if she felt any sympathy for her father-in-law it had been destroyed by his reversion back to the catholic religion. It also strengthened her resolve; she knew she would never do the same even if it meant it could save her life. She was disgusted by her father-in-law's last-minute desertion of the protestant faith, to her he placed his soul in extreme danger, her intolerance of those who did not share her feelings about religion was becoming more and more zealous.

Back at the Tower, the earl of Warwick went back to his brothers and Jane remained with the Constable. With not much to stimulate her mind she turned her attention to her religious writings but she needed to take heed because Queen Mary was just as zealous as she was and if she was not careful they would be at loggerheads and that would do Jane's cause no good. The queen had already started to reverse Edward VI's religious changes by implementing the Act of Repeal in her first parliament. The catholic faith began to be restored and soon Jane had new neighbours, Protestant leaders Bishop Hugh Latimer and the Archbishop of Canterbury Thomas Cranmer, had been arrested and imprisoned, both would be executed by Mary.

Amidst the trials and sentences King Edward VI was laid to rest in the Henry VII Lady Chapel in Westminster Abbey on 8 August. His body had laid at rest at Greenwich and was moved from there to Whitehall and then onto the Abbey where the walls were draped in black. His coffin had been adorned in blue velvet with a life like effigy of Edward with the crown and sceptre. The ceremony was performed by the archbishop of Canterbury as per the rites of the reformist religion as agreed by Mary, she was willing to allow her brother to be laid to rest in his chosen way. The mourners that lined the streets grieved deeply for their young king who was taken from them far too young. Edward had signified so much promise for the county but with him went the hope of another glorious Tudor king. In his wake came a Tudor queen albeit not the queen Edward had chosen. Edward's reign did not leave a lasting effect on his people, he did not have an imposing reign like his grandfather, father and half-sisters instead, what perhaps he is known for was his nomination of Jane as queen and the 'nine-day queen' title that cemented her place in the history of England.

With two women both utterly convinced their religion is the true one, both zealous in their beliefs, religion once again came at the forefront of English psyche. The continuing arguments between Catholicism and Protestantism were raging and the casualties would be vast on both sides. Jane continued in her confinement, awaiting Mary's pardon but events that were once again beyond her control began to take over and would prove to be catastrophic.

Chapter 12

The Trial

Queen Mary was still under immense pressure to take action against Jane and the Dudley brothers but still she refused to be drawn on the subject. Whilst it showed her kind and tolerant side it also showed her weaknesses because it highlighted a lack of authority on her part. In order to stave off criticism she ordered the trial of Jane, Guildford and his brothers Ambrose and Henry. This news must have come as a concern to the Suffolks and the Duchess of Northumberland who were under the impression a pardon would be forthcoming soon. The trial date was set for 13 November 1553.

The trial was to be held in the Great Hall at the Guildhall and once again the Duke of Norfolk would preside over proceedings along with fifteen other men, all appointed by the queen, all Catholics. It was to be held in public and it has been estimated nearly 1000 people crammed into the hall to witness the trial.

Jane was dressed all in black and was collected from her rooms and went to join her husband and brothers-in-law Ambrose and Henry and Thomas Cranmer. They were escorted to the Guildhall by the Constable of the Tower and Lord Chamberlain, Sir John Gage. The accused were led by soldiers, one holding an axe pointing away from them which shows they had not yet stood trial. Should they be found guilty and sentenced to death, the return journey would see the axe turned inwards. The journey of just one mile was taken on foot and as she made her way through the guard lined streets Jane held her prayer book open in front of her enabling her to read from it throughout the journey. The impression of a young pious girl was not lost on the onlookers but Jane was absorbed in her belief that God was her true saviour and her faith stood firm. As they arrived they entered the overcrowded hall where Jane stood beside her husband but in truth she was once again just a pawn of men. She again had no power to affect proceedings that involved her, instead she cut a sombre figure, a diminutive young girl dressed all in black.

They all stood accused of high treason and Jane was tried under her married name Jane Dudley, no comment was made of her rank or status she was simply Guildford Dudley's wife, nothing more, nothing less. As the trial commenced they were each accused of being rebels against Queen Mary and the evidence presented was condemning. Jane and Guildford had entered the Tower of London, she assumed the title of Queen and even tried on the crown for size. It was stated she had 'falsely and treacherously assumed and took up for herself the title and power of the queen of this kingdom of England' More damming though, she had signed documents as 'Jane the Quene' none of the accused were given the opportunity to defend themselves. If Jane had it would have been difficult to explain away her actions once she entered the Tower, the time to refuse the crown would surely have been before then. We know from our privileged view point that Jane was forced to take the crown. She was given no option to decline, for if she had her parents may well have disowned her. But the men sat in judgement against her have only the facts as they have been presented. They have seen Jane take control of the Tower, raise an army against Mary and accept the crown jewels. All three defendants pleaded guilty to the charges laid before them and in doing so signed their own death warrants, to avoid death they would have to hope Mary would continue to treat them leniently.

When it came to sentencing, the men came first:

'Each of them should so be dragged and there hung and each of them hung, and laid out rotting on the ground, and their interior organs should be brought outside their stomachs, and as these rot they should be burned. And their heads should be cut off, and their bodies, and any those of them, should be divided into four quarters should be placed where the Queen wishes them to be assigned'

For Jane, the following chilling punishment was given:

'The said Jane be led off by the said Constable of the said Tower of London to the prison of the said Queen within the same Tower, and then on the order of the Queen herself led to Tower Hill and there be burned, or the head cut off, as it will then please the Queen'

The sentence was passed down by the chief justice Sir Richard Morgan and later stories tell us he went insane following his condemnation of Jane. He claimed her ghost haunted him which led him to later kill himself although there is no evidence to back this up. Throughout the trial Jane remained calm and emotionless; it is hard to understand why because many people in this situation would have shown at least a flicker of emotion, they would cry and plead for leniency but not Jane, she took her sentence in and remained impassive. Maybe she had resigned herself to this fate, she had spent many weeks in the Tower contemplating her eventual fate, she must have known if she stood trial and pleaded guilty then the only one outcome was available. Alternatively, she may have continued to hope Mary would carry on showing her good favour and not carry out the sentence after all she had only done the bidding of others and Mary understood her position in the whole saga. Like most other 16-year-olds she may just have been too petrified over her fate to show emotion. On the return journey to the Tower the axe was turned to point inwards showing they had been found guilty and condemned to death. No date was set for the executions and they all went back to their cells and life carried on as it had before. Jane continued to find solace from reading her Bible and reading and studying books that were made available to her.

Jane's intensity in her religion came very much from her father and he was beginning to make comments about Mary's changes. Like many reformers he was upset that Edward's reforms had been swept aside and his voice on this matter was getting louder. Considering he was under house arrest and under the threat of re-arrest, speaking out against Mary was a very unwise thing to do, even more so given his daughter's recent conviction for high treason. With the onset of a return to Catholicism many people gave an outward appearance of renouncing Protestantism in favour of a return to the old religion but many did this just to stay safe. Suffolk and his family were some of these people and this news undoubtedly made Mary happy. It would also have gone some way in helping the family return to favour but he was known as being a devout reformer, just like Jane, and the likelihood of his conversion being genuine was rather stretched. Remarkably, Mary believed him and gave him a full pardon for his involvement in putting Jane on the throne. It also went some way in winning her freedom which would be almost guaranteed, all the family had to do was remain patient and in time Jane would be released. Or so they believed.

With the trial over and done with and the sentences handed down, focus now turned to Queen Mary and her potential bridegroom. Naturally the queen looked towards her family in Spain and the Holy Roman Empire for guidance on a possible match and it was finally agreed that the son of Emperor Charles V, Philip II would be the lucky man. Mary may have felt happy in her choice as it provided her with a union with her beloved Spain and it would bring untold happiness and riches to England. Unfortunately for the queen the people were not happy at the prospect of having a foreign prince sat beside their queen on the throne. The common feeling was the country would get engulfed by Spain and just become an outpost of the empire. It was felt England would get embroiled in wars it did not want and with politics it did not agree with but most importantly it would mean a full return to Rome and the catholic church. Mary listened to her people's grievances but decided not to take them on board, she was in love with the handsome Philip and instead she forged ahead with her plans, unaware of the damage she was about to do. For Jane, she would have no idea what impact Mary's decision was going to have on her and her family, no one could have predicted what would happen next.

But that was in the future, for the time being the good news came that she, along with the Dudley brothers, were to be given more freedom. The order came that they were to be permitted to walk in the Tower gardens for exercise and fresh air. Jane would enjoy walks in the Queen's gardens and out on Tower Hill but there is no evidence to suggest she crossed paths with Guildford or his brothers. But this was surely a sign that a full pardon was coming, this could be seen as the first step in acclimatising the prisoners to the outside world again. As the year of 1553 began to draw to a close there was every reason to be hopeful. Brydges urged Jane to be so and she took on board what her new friend had to say. They had formed a friendly relationship during her stay at the Tower and he later commented that he enjoyed her company, lively debates and eating together. As the festive season came and went the Grey family would have felt Jane's absence more keenly but surely it was now just a matter of time before she would be reunited with her family back at Sheen. The family was back in favour, all they had to do was keep their heads down, keep quiet and not involve themselves in anything controversial. After all, their daughter's life hung on the very outcome of their behaviour. Unfortunately for Jane, she had the hapless Henry Grey as her father and he was always liable to go head-long into a plan without much thought of the consequences.

Chapter 13

The Final Downfall

As the year of 1554 dawned there was an air of mixed optimism and dread sweeping through the court. The queen's marriage negotiations were well under way, for the 37-year-old to land herself a groom of just 26 must have given her a huge sense of pride but there were some sticking points. Those being mainly the fact her councillors and people were for the most part dead set against the match. For the queen, she had seriously underestimated just how much her people were opposed to a union with Spain but the English had always been good at letting their feelings be known. Before long Mary had yet another rebellion to deal with, except this time she was on the other side and was having to defend her position.

Suffolk had spent much of the Christmas period in discussion over a rebellion with politician and rebel Thomas Wyatt who was adamant the Spanish marriage should not go ahead. It was his view that the threat of Rome should be expelled at whatever cost. Henry was also against this idea as he saw it as a threat to the reformist ideals that he had worked so hard to instil in England. Despite giving an outward appearance of having converted back to Catholicism he clearly had not, he was too much of a hardcore reformer to ever contemplate this. Suffolk was also angered by the fact he had not been given a place on the newly formed government, it seemed lost on him that whilst his daughter sat in the Tower as a convicted traitor his chances of being in government were slim and that's before we take into account his own role in the plot that brought his family so low. The Duke of Suffolk comes across as a man who never really grasped the reality of a situation, his bafflement over his omission from court and now his reluctance to see the danger he was putting his family in with his latest plotting seem utterly lost on him. Jane was just one swing of an axe away from losing her head. Not content with the damage he had already done to his family, he also enlisted the support of his brothers Lord Thomas Grey and Lord John Grey in his quest, embroiling his family even further into the intrigue. Frances was absolutely against his plans and must have felt exasperated by her husbands misguided and deluded plans, it was unlikely her grovelling to Mary would be as successful again, if the plan failed there really was only one outcome but Suffolk heeded no warnings and threw his hat in with the rebels.

The aim of the rebellion was to replace Mary with Elizabeth and in doing so stop the country returning the Rome and the Papacy. Elizabeth was a committed Protestant and would be more than likely to marry an English man, with many suggesting Edward Courtenay, Earl of Devon to be the best match. She was younger and seemed to be more pliable than Mary, she had proved no one's fool but they felt Elizabeth to be easier to negotiate with, she was not as strict with her religion as Mary and could push the Protestant religion further than ever before. It is interesting to note that no one suggested releasing Jane from the Tower and placing her back on the throne, it was clear lessons had been learnt from before. The rebels knew the people would want Elizabeth and if they wanted the plan to succeed then she would have to be queen. There may have been a deal struck with Suffolk that if the plan succeeded then Jane was to be fully pardoned and released from the Tower and returned to her family. I would like to think he thought enough about his daughter to make this suggestion and if he didn't then maybe Frances would have.

The Courtenay family had royal blood in its veins, Edward's paternal grandmother was Princess Catherine of York, sister to Elizabeth's grandmother Elizabeth of York and queen consort of Henry VII. Their royal links had often placed the family in trouble and they found themselves incarcerated in the Tower on the orders of Henry VIII after been accused of conspiring with Cardinal Reginald Pole to lead a Catholic uprising. His father was executed for his role in the 'Exeter Conspiracy' whilst his mother was released he remained locked up due to his being the great-grandson of King Edward IV and a potential heir to the house of York, meaning he was a direct threat to the House of Tudor. It was only when Mary ascended the throne that he finally got released and she treated him well, raising him to the earldom of Devon and making him a Knight of the Bath, he was even given a prominent role in her coronation. There was talk that Courtenay was a potential choice of husband for Mary but when she chose Philip over him he switched his sights to Elizabeth. Did he feel resentful at the rejection so much that he was willing to join the rebels? It certainly appears that way. He had only been out of the Tower six months and yet here he was trying to gain control of the throne by marrying Mary's half-sister. It seems Henry VIII and Edward VI were right in keeping him locked up, it looked like he wanted to make trouble.

The Wyatt Rebellion, as it became known, was led by a group of nobles including the Duke of Suffolk, Sir James Croft from Herefordshire, Sir Peter Carew of Devon and Sir Thomas Wyatt, a landowner and former soldier from Kent. His father was the famed poet Thomas Wyatt the Elder who had at one time been incarcerated in the Tower over an alleged affair with Anne Boleyn, he was later released. Wyatt the Younger had served in the army under Henry VIII and had fought alongside the Spanish in the war against the French. It is thought his hatred of Spain came from this time and it was clear he still harboured that resentment to the point of being ready to kill. In terms of his religion, it appears to be rather ambiguous, he certainly had protestant leanings but like so many others he gave the outward appearance of being catholic to please the sovereign.

The plan was that each leader was to lead an uprising in four regions, the Midlands, Kent, the West Country and the Welsh Borders and they would then all converge on London. On the face of it this seems to be an impressive plan, the idea of co-ordinated simultaneous revolts was to cause confusion in the government as they would not know which to put down first. The royal troops would not be able to resist all four uprisings at once which would mean one of the groups would probably be successful. But in reality having so many groups spread over such a wide distance was bound to cause issues. For one, communication between each faction could take days, any change to a plan could be disastrous. The French got involved too as it was in their interests to stop a Spaniard from sitting on the throne of England so they offered to block any Spanish ships in the English Channel that may come to Mary's aid or more importantly let Philip in. The initial date for the attack was going to be Palm Sunday, 18 March 1554 but unfortunately for the rebels, news of the plot reached the ears of the Imperial Ambassador Simon Renard and he related the plot to the Lord Chancellor Bishop Stephen Gardner who moved quickly. He bought in Sir Peter Carew and Edward Courtney, Earl of Devon for questioning as his name had been specifically mentioned by Renard. Devon admitted the there was a planned uprising against the queen. Thomas Grey heard that the details had been leaked and rode to Sheen to tell his brother Suffolk that the rebellion needed to be brought forward. Each man had managed to return to their estates and on 25 January, with everyone in position, and backed by many men, Wyatt raised his standard at Maidstone signalling the beginning of the rebellion.

The rebellion did not get off to the best start, Carew failed to raise Devon and instead fled to France. On 29 January the duke of Suffolk arrived at Leicester in his full armour, he demanded the gates to the city be closed, when inside he read a proclamation which railed against the Spanish marriage, he was adamant he meant no harm to Queen Mary and would kill any man that did. On the afternoon of 30 January, he left Leicester but he had only managed to raise several hundred men and when they arrived at Coventry, they were refused entry. He was now aware that Huntingdon's men were on their tail and not far from Coventry he knew the game was up and fled to his estate Astley, Warwickshire.

When they arrived, he urged his followers to flee, he gave them money and bid them goodbye. He changed out of his armour and made plans to evade Huntingdon's men. He made feeble attempts to hide and when the guards came looking an estate worker named Nicholas Lawrence guided the earl of Huntingdon's officers to a hollowed-out tree where they found the duke hiding inside. When he had started to proclaim that Jane was the true queen he did nothing but cause further harm and damage to his daughter. The Grey brothers had managed to flee but John was found hiding nearby under bales of hay, Thomas had managed to head towards the Welsh borders but was soon found and brought back to Coventry where they were proclaimed traitors. Suffolk wrote down his own confession but at no point did he show any remorse for his participation in the uprising. He seems to have been incapable of understanding any threatening situation he was in. Suffolk and his brothers arrived at the Tower of London on 10 February. If he was relying on Frances to smooth things over for him yet again then he was sadly mistaken, there was to be no pardon this time.

It looked like Wyatt was going to have to carry this attack on his own, he had managed to raise and impressive 4000 men which caused London great concern. The ageing Duke of Norfolk was sent by Mary to put down the rebellion as Wyatt approached Rochester but he failed to do so and retreated back to London. Many of Norfolk's men went over to Wyatt as they marched on London. It appears Wyatt's men were well drilled, many probably seasoned soldiers, they knew what they're doing. With no obstacles in his way London all of a sudden became exposed, Mary was advised to flee the capital, but others urged her to stay but if she did then the defence of London needed to be ramped up, and quickly. The men in charge of defending London were the Earl of Pembroke and Lord Edward Clinton. They raised 500 troops and 200 horse, this was fraught with uncertainty, Pembroke had been a onetime supporter of Northumberland and even though Mary had pardoned him she and the council did not know with any certainty how far his loyalty stretched. The thought at the Tower; was this another attack by them to get Jane back on the throne?

Initially, many thought it was, there was no consideration given to Elizabeth being the target for the throne, for all intents and purposes it looked like Mary had been duped into another threat to her crown by Suffolk and his supporters. This caused huge concern to Mary and led to her councillors offering to enter into negotiations with the rebels but Wyatt refused the offer and said his aim was to capture the queen and hold her hostage in the Tower. He boldly demanded complete control of the Tower of London, including its armoury and of the Queen herself, angered by this bold request Mary rallied the people of London to her cause when she gave an impassioned speech at the Guildhall on 1 February. Wyatt delayed in making his advance to London which gave the government the opportunity to shore up the city's defences even further, and when he and his forces arrived in Southwark on 3 February they found the city well defended.

They were unable to cross the River Thames at London Bridge due to it being heavily guarded by Mary's supporters. Not to be deterred, Wyatt travelled further down river to Kingston hoping to cross there but again, the bridge had been damaged and his men were forced to rebuild it. They managed to cross to the north bank of the Thames where they faced little opposition, they turned eastwards and advanced on the city. The resistance came as the rebels approached Ludgate, trouble started and they split up but many got trapped amongst the narrow streets and panic set in. Wyatt was quickly captured and instantly sent to the Tower of London with the other leaders. Mary's capacity for forgiveness and pardons was exhausted and she demanded swift action and even though she pardoned many of the rebels a total of ninety were executed.

It has been suggested Wyatt was tortured in an attempt to implicate Elizabeth in the plot, he refused to confirm this but Mary was not satisfied and arranged for her sister to be brought to London for questioning. Elizabeth was horrified to discover she had been implicated and suffered a mental collapse when she heard she was to be arrested on the orders of her sister. From her rooms in the Tower Jane must have heard the panic and commotion and later the arrival of prisoners. She may have known what the ruckus was about, Brydges may have told her and then relayed to her the role her father was having in it all. How this would all impact her she had no idea; all she could do at this point was sit and wait for further news.

Sadly, Suffolk's actions had signed his daughter's and Guildford's death warrant, he had betrayed her in the most callous and destructive way. Can he have even thought of her at all during this time? It is hard to defend his actions in any way, during the Northumberland uprising you could argue Suffolk was weak and allowed himself to be manipulated by a more powerful man but here, what was his excuse, other than being a selfish and stupid man.

But what of Jane? It is unclear as to whether she was fully aware that her father's actions and his arrest would bring the axe down on her, she must have clung to the hope that Mary would still be lenient towards her but the Grey family could no longer take advantage of the queen's kind nature, time had run out.

Chapter 14

The Execution

The realisation that Jane was always going to be a focal point of rebellion had finally dawned on the queen and she had been left with no choice but to sign her death warrant, the punishment was commuted to beheading for both Jane and Guildford. It was not just her royal blood that meant Jane stood close to the throne but also her staunch Protestantism, she was a well-known figurehead for reform and those two things combined meant Mary could not allow her to live if she wanted to return England to Rome. It was a very reluctant queen that condemned her kinswoman to death but to be fair she had been far more lenient than her father would have been but there was now nothing she could do to protect Jane from the scaffold. The blame had to squarely lay at the feet of her father, had Suffolk not engaged with the rebels and taken such misguided action and continued to call for Jane to be crowned queen, in time Jane could have been released quietly back to her family. The irony is her father should have been the one man she could rely on to protect her and keep her safe, but thanks to no fault of her own she was condemned to die as a traitor.

The speculated date she was told she was to die is 7 February she is said to have taken the news calmly and with dignity, despite her tender years. Jane was acting with true regality and far beyond her years. Her execution was initially scheduled for morning on the 9 February but Mary decided to send her own personal chaplain Dr John Feckenham to visit Jane in a last-minute attempt to covert her to Catholicism. He felt he would be successful given the time; Mary sanctioned him three days to achieve this but both had seriously underestimated Jane's dedication to her religion. Was the queen hoping to find a reprieve for Jane? If she converted then she could no longer be the figurehead for protestants and maybe her life could be spared, but neither did she want Jane dying a protestant martyr. It was clear Mary was in great pains over Jane's death, if she gave little thought to her life she would have had her executed much earlier but out of family loyalty she resisted. The queen would not have wanted her soul on her conscience and felt if she could not save her mortal body then maybe she could save her soul from eternal damnation. Given her anguish at facing death, Jane listened to what Feckenham had to say but told him early on he was wasting his time, she was prepared to die and nothing he could say, no argument he could brook would divert her from her religion. Religion had been the one mainstay in her life, when she was little and alone, when she could turn to no person, when her parents deserted her in the Tower of London she still had her God. But Feckenham remained determined to try and he visited Jane over the next three days, they had heated arguments with each having a ready answer for the other but what Mary and Feckenham failed to realise was Jane was not going to concede her religion because it was all she had left.

It was unfair of Mary to expect Jane to change her religion to Catholicism as she had never known that religion, she had been born and raised a protestant so to suggest she switch to save her life was unfounded. Feckenham told Jane how sorry he was for her sad situation, he marvelled at how calm she was in the face of death but to Jane it was God's plan for her and she was happy to follow his plan. She had been callously used by selfish power-hungry men, men who should have been protecting her. She had been let down, used and had her freedom denied her all for a crown she never wanted, she was damned if she was going to let another man take something from her. She dug in and won the argument, Feckenham left her with a sense of admiration and respect, impressed that someone so young could face death with such a sense of resolve. Jane was going to her death a Protestant martyr.

A new date for the executions came, the 12 February would see Jane and her husband Guildford finally climb the scaffold to their fate.

He would be taken out to Tower Hill, to the same scaffold his father lost his head on just months earlier, whilst Jane would be beheaded within the privacy of the Tower complex given her royal status.

As her last full day on earth dawned she would have been able to hear and see the construction of the scaffold, the time had finally come to prepare for death, there was no more time left to hope for a pardon. She sat to write her last letters, no doubt she sent one to her mother but no copy survives if she did, we do know however that she wrote to her sister Katherine. She sent her a copy of the New Testament in Greek, in it she wrote 'rejoice as I do, good sister, that I shall be delivered of this corruption, for I am assured, that I shall, for losing of a mortal life, win an immortal life'. Next came her father, being prisoners, they were not permitted to meet face to face. There have been questions raised over whether she wrote a letter at all and many doubts have been raised over the validity of the letter she is said to have written. In it she condemns him for her downfall but this is at odds with the loving note she wrote in her prayer book in which she forgives him his role in her death. There is no solid evidence to support this letter as being written by Jane and the fact it was only 'discovered' ten years after her death makes it all the more questionable. I feel to gauge Jane's true feelings for her father we should look to the note she wrote for him in her beloved prayer book. She wrote:

> 'The Lord comfort your grace and that in his word wherein all creatures only are to be comforted and though it hath pleased god to take away two of your children yet think not I most humbly beseech your grace that you have lost them but trust that we by losing this mortal life have won an immortal life and I for my part as I have honoured your grace in this life will pray for you in another. Your humble daughter, Jane Dudley'

After she had written her note the prayer book was then passed to Guildford who also wrote a message for his father-in-law. Guildford requested a final meeting between himself and Jane but she declined, she may have seen no point in pro-longing their agony and she reassured her husband they would soon see each other in another life 'and live bound by dissolvable ties'. It is hard to determine what kind of marriage they had, they were both reluctant to wed and were young too, it was clearly a marriage to please others but maybe they did build some kind of relationship that was kind and loving. As they sat alone in the Tower awaiting their fate I hope they were able to offer each other some element of support, love and reassurance. Regardless of what she thought of him, he deserved to die no less than she did, he was just as much a victim of his father's machinations for power as she was and in that they were united. And with that she turned her mind to her final prayers.

As the dawn of 12 February 1534 broke over London the weather was bright but chilly with a light frost on the ground. Guildford was to die first at 10am, Jane watched from her window as the guards came for him and escorted him the short distance to Tower Hill, he was led by Brydges and was then passed over into the custody of the Sheriff of London Thomas Offley. He climbed the steps of the scaffold with no resistance, knelt and said his prayers and laid his neck on the block. The executioner severed his head from his body with just one stroke. His body was placed in a cart, his bloody head wrapped in cloth and place beside him, the cart trundled back to the Tower, over the cobbles and on to the chapel of St Peter ad Vincula. Guildford Dudley was just 18 years old when he died so bravely.

Given her prominent location in the Tower, Jane was able to watch as her husband's broken body was brought back to the Tower, only minutes before she had witnessed him walk to his death, now she knew it was her turn.

Brydges came to collect Jane from her rooms shortly after Guildford's return, she bequeathed him her prayer book, a sign of the close bond that had grown over the months whilst she was in his care, she wrote a message in it for him to read. She left her rooms for the last time, escorted by Brydges, Elizabeth Tilney and Mistress Ellen. She carried her beloved prayer book to the scaffold, taking comfort from the words she read, she walked calmy and remained composed at all times. She reached the foot of the stairs to find Feckenham waiting for her, he requested to be there as a friend and in no other capacity, she agreed and climbed the stairs unfalteringly. A small crowd had gathered to see her final moments and the mood was sombre and sad but for Jane it was finally her moment to speak, for her voice to be heard. The crowd fell silent as Jane began her final speech.

'Good people, I am come hither to die, and by a law I am condemned to the same. The fact, indeed, against the queen's highness was unlawful, and the consenting thereunto by me: but touching the procurement and desire thereof by me or on my behalf, I do wash my hands thereof in innocency, before God, and the face of you, good Christian people, this day. I pray you all, good Christian people, to bear me witness that I die a true Christian woman, and that I look to be saved by none other mean, but only by the mercy of God in the merits of the blood of his only son Jesus Christ: and I confess, when I did know of the word of God I neglected the same, loved myself and the world, and therefore this plague or punishment is happily and worthily happened unto me for my sins: and yet I thank god of his goodness that he hath thus given me a time and respect to repent. And now, good people, while I am alive, I pray you to assist me with your prayers.'

After she had finished, she knelt, opened her prayer book and turned to Feckenham asking if she should read Psalm 51, yes he agreed and she recited her final prayer:

"Oh Lord, thou God and father of my life! hear me, poor and desolate women, which flyeth unto three only,

131

in all troubles and miseries. Thou, O Lord, art the only defender and deliverer of those that put their trust in thee, and, therefore, I, being defiled with sin, encumbered with affliction, unquieted with troubles, wrapped in cares, overwhelmed with miseries, vexed with temptations, and grievously tormented with the long imprisonment of this vile mass of clay, my sinful body, do come unto three, O merciful Saviour, craving they mercy and help, without the which so little hope of deliverance is left, that I may utterly despair of my liberty. Albeit, it is expedient, that seeing our life standeth upon trying, we should be visited some time with some adversity, whereby we might both be tried whether we be of thy flock or no; and also know thee and ourselves the better; yet thou that saidst thou wouldst not suffer us to be tempted above our power, be merciful unto me, now a miserable wretch, I beseech thee; which, with Solomon, do cry unto thee, humbly desiring thee, that I may neither be too much puffed up with prosperity, neither too much depressed with adversity; lest I, being too full, should deny thee, my God; or being too low brought, should despair and blaspheme thee, my Lord and Saviour. O merciful God, consider my misery, best known unto thee; and be thou now unto me a strong tower of defence, I humbly require thee. Suffer me not to be tempted above my power, but either be thou a deliverer unto me out of this great misery, or else give me grace patiently to bear thy heavy hand and sharp correction. It was thy right hand that delivered the people of Israel out of the hands of Pharoah, which for the space of four hundred years did oppress them, and keep them in bondage; let it therefore likewise seem good to thy fatherly goodness, to deliver me, sorrowful wretch, for whom thy son Christ shed his precious blood on the cross, out of this miserable captivity and bondage, wherein I am now. How long wilt thou be absent – for ever? Oh, Lord! hast thou forgotten to be gracious, and hast thou shut up thy loving kindness in displeasure? wilt thou be no more entreated? Is thy mercy clear gone for ever, and thy promise come utterly to an end for everyone? why dost thou make so long tarrying? shall I despair of thy mercy? Oh God! far be that from me; I am thy workmanship, created in Christ Jesus; give me grace therefore to tarry thy leisure, and patiently to bear thy works, assuredly knowing, that as thou canst, so thou wilt deliver me, when it shall please thee, nothing doubting or mistrusting thy goodness towards me; for thou knowest better what is good for me than I do; therefore do with me in all things what thou wilt, and plague me what way thou wilt. Only in the mean time, arm me, I beseech thee, with they armour, that I may stand fast, my loins being girded about with verity, having on the breast-plate of righteousness, and shod with the shoes prepared by the gospel of peace; above all things, taking to me the shield of faith, wherewith I may be able to quench all the fiery darts of the wicked; and taking the helmet of salvation, and the sword of thy spirit, which is thy most holy word; praying always, with all manner of prayer and supplication, that I may refer myself wholly to thy will, abiding thy pleasure, and comforting myself in those troubles that it shall please thee to send me; seeing such troubles be profitable for me, and seeing I am assuredly persuaded that it cannot but be well all thou doest. Hear me, O merciful Father, for his sake, whom thou wouldest should be a sacrifice for my sins; to whom with thee and the Holy Ghost, be all honour and glory. Amen!'

Upon finishing she turned to Elizabeth Tilney and handed over her gloves and handkerchief and then passed her beloved prayer book to Thomas Brydges, brother to her friend. She then proceeded to untie the laces of her gown, batting away the offered assistance from the executioner to help, he was not to touch her until the very last moment. Instead, he knelt before her and asked for forgiveness for what he was about to do, she gave it willingly. She then turned to her ladies for assistance, they tearfully loosened her hair and then the executioner approached and asked Jane to stand on the straw in front of the block. 'I pray you dispatch me quickly' she says to him as she knelt then turning she asked the him, 'will you take it off before I lay me down? 'No madam' came the response. Her weeping ladies tied the handkerchief over her eyes, bringing nothing but darkness to her world. As Jane took one last glance at the world, what did she see? Did she take any comfort from any friendly faces in the crowd? Unable to see she started to panic, she realised she was too far from the block 'What shall I do? Where is it?' she asked as her hands were grasping the thin air in front of her until someone stepped forward and guided her to the block. She then laid her head down and said 'Lord Jesus, into thy hands I commend my spirit!' and with one swing of the axe Lady Jane Grey's head was severed from her body. With that, her world finally went dark forever.

Lady Jane Grey, one time Queen of England, was just 16 years old when she died so bravely at the hand of the executioner and she was celebrated across Europe both during and after her death for her devout Protestant beliefs.

Chapter 15

The Aftermath

Jane's body remained on the bloodied scaffold all day before it was removed for burial alongside Guildford's in St Peter ad Vincula, the actual location is not known although there is a Victorian memorial to her at the foot of the chancel. But Jane's death was not the end of the story, her father had his fate to face and the family had to forge some kind of path forward. Henry Grey, Duke of Suffolk's trial took place on 22 February, he was taken from the Tower to Westminster Hall where he was charged with high treason, he pleaded not guilty. He stated it was not treason to defend ones country from foreign interference (relating to the Spanish marriage). He was found guilty and sentenced to death, he made the return trip to the Tower by barge and was executed at 9am on 23 February on Tower Hill but his execution was not without some controversy.

He was accompanied to the scaffold by Hugh Weston, the queens chaplain but the sermon he gave attacked the beliefs that Suffolk had defended so passionately which naturally angered him and as he climbed the steps of the scaffold he turned and pushed Weston away but he had a firm grip of Suffolk causing them both to fall down the steps to the foot of the scaffold. There was to be a further clash with Weston as he declared it was the queens wish that he attend Suffolk at this time. Suffolk stood and calmed himself, he relented and climbed the steps once more and when he reached the top he asked for the queen's forgiveness which Weston gave. Suffolk read a psalm after which he gave his cap and neckerchief to the executioner, who then knelt and asked Suffolk for his forgiveness, which Suffolk granted. Incredibly at that point one of Suffolk's creditors stepped forward to ask what was to be done about the outstanding payments he was owed; he was quickly removed and Suffolk proceeded to remove his gown and doublet. Just like his daughter had done just days before, he tied a handkerchief around his eyes and knelt, recited the Lord's Prayer and placed his neck on the block, his head was removed with just one strike of the axe.

Suffolk's brother Thomas Grey was also executed but their brother John received a pardon possibly due to his catholic family links. The charge of treason meant all the Suffolks' property and wealth was forfeited to the crown leaving Frances, Katherine and Mary in dire straits. Frances had seen sense and did not approach the queen to ask for a reprieve because she knew he would not be pardoned twice, but she did ask that she could forgive the crimes of her family and perhaps restore some of the property and lands. Frances had no choice but to look to the future for the sake of her two daughters, Katherine was 13 and Mary just 9 when their sister and father were executed. They lived as Catholics despite being protestant and in time Mary forgave them and restored some of the land in Leicestershire back to Frances. She even invited her cousin and daughters back to court. Frances entered the Queen's Privy Chamber and the girls thrived on court life. There was talk of Frances remarrying, Edward Courtenay's name was bandied about but the fact the Privy Council were involving themselves with Frances was interesting, did they see her as a potential heir to Mary? Elizabeth and Mary were not getting on and it seemed like a natural progression to look to Frances although it was another Tudor cousin who briefly became Mary's preferred heir. Margaret Douglas, Countess of Lennox had been close to Mary and Frances since their childhood, having the three cousins together must have brought happiness and joy to Mary who finally had people around her she could love and who in returned loved her too.

When it came down to remarrying, the choice of groom was a surprise. Frances remarried in 1555 not long after her husband's death, the man in question was Adrian Stokes, her Master of the Horse, a former soldier, a protestant and commoner with whom Queen Mary approved of. She had married far below her rank and by doing so had removed herself from the line of succession. It would be a move Elizabeth would find abhorrent but ensured she would never be a threat to her throne. But after all the heartaches it did not matter, Frances was happy and she spent more time away from court. Sadly, she suffered numerous miscarriages and still births and as a result her health began to falter. Mary went home with her mother but the ever-vivacious Katherine stayed at court and became one of its brightest stars.

Frances Grey, Duchess of Suffolk, daughter to the former French Queen and granddaughter to King Henry VII died on 20 November 1559 aged 42 years old with her daughters by her side. Her funeral was held on 5 December at Westminster Abbey with the full honours that befitted a member of the royal house of Tudor. As her surviving eldest daughter and dressed in black Katherine performed the role of chief mourner; with Mary following closely behind. It was a protestant funeral held in English and she was laid to rest in St Edmunds Chapel and four years later Stokes erected an alabaster monument to his late wife, the inscription reads:

> Nor grace, nor splendor, nor a royal name,
> Nor widespread fame can aught avail;
> All, all have vanished here.
> True worth alone Survives the funeral pyre and silent tomb

History has not been kind to Frances thanks in part to Ascham's account of Jane's accusations of ill-treatment and of her abandonment of Jane following her ill-fated queenship. It is hard to understand her actions, it cannot be solely down to a lack of love or her maternal skills for she had two other daughters who appear to have had a kinder relationship with her. Just prior to her death Frances was in the process of trying to secure permission from Elizabeth I for Katherine to marry her love, the Earl of Hertford, which suggests the two enjoyed a close relationship sadly Frances's death meant no official agreement leaving the 19-year-old Katherine devastated.

It is difficult to interpret exactly what Frances was like as a mother, Katherine and Mary never spoke of ill-treatment and seemed close to her, especially as they grew older, was Frances simply trying to make amends, making sure she did not lose another child, was it simply her guilt that drove her to be a better mother than she had been to Jane.

The irony of Jane's death is that neither Mary or Elizabeth had children so Jane, or her sisters, had they still been alive at the time of Elizabeth's death in 1603, would have inherited the throne anyway. The Grey sisters were still a threat to Mary's throne, they had the same right to inherit that Jane did but there never seemed to be any talk of putting Katherine on the throne in Mary's place but perhaps that was because they had already tried and it hadn't worked, there was no need to risk any potential bloodshed.

The move to execute Jane and Guildford was not a popular one, it showed Mary to be weak and unable to make a decision and the popularity she felt at the time of her accession had dwindled away. Her marriage plans and her husband were detested and her need to punish reformers left her with a reputation as 'Bloody Mary'. Mary's reign was not a glorious one, she was desperate to return the country to Rome, her Spanish husband was not trusted and spent very little time in England, she lost England's last foot hold in Europe by losing Calais and her health often plagued her. She failed to produce the much-needed male heir, despite thinking she was pregnant on more than one occasion, she suffered phantom pregnancies and died a bitter and unhappy woman at the age of 42 after reigning for just over five years. Mary named her younger half-sister Elizabeth as her heir and there was no threat from any quarter and she took her throne unimpeded but that was not to say the Grey sisters would not be a cause for concern to her too throughout her reign. Katherine would make her clandestine marriage to Edward Seymour, son of the Lord Protector Somerset, without Elizabeth's approval and when she found herself pregnant she begged Robert Dudley for help. Elizabeth was furious to find her cousin had ignored royal protocol and threw her in the Tower where Katherine would give birth to a baby son,

Lord Beauchamp. Hertford soon joined his wife as prisoner but thanks to a kindly guard the two were allowed to meet, Katherine fell pregnant again and delivered another baby boy. Elizabeth was apoplectic with rage, she announced the children, who had incredibly strong claims for the throne as illegitimate and separated Katherine from her husband permanently. She was put under house arrest but her heartbreak caused an early death and she died aged just 27 years old, many romantically believed she died of a broken heart but it was more than likely from consumption.

Mary Grey fared no better when it came to being happy in the love department. She met and fell in love and married without the queens permission as well. She fell in love with Thomas Keyes, he was a sergeant porter to the queen and stood at over 6ft 8" which compared to Mary's miniscule 4ft 8" led to many cruel barbs. Elizabeth once again annulled a Grey marriage and Mary was put under house arrest; Thomas was sent to the Fleet Prison. Following his death and her release Mary moved from house to house not feeling welcome anywhere. Eventually she entered Elizabeth's household as a Maid of Honour and stood as the next in line to the throne, although this claim was never truly taken seriously. Lady Mary Grey died on 20 April 1578 aged just 33 years old. She was laid to rest in her mother's tomb at Westminster Abbey.

The younger of Henry Grey's daughters certainly showed traits of his, both seemed to be wreckless girls who never fully thought through the consequences of their actions. It is almost as if they did not take seriously how close they stood to the throne, had the death of their elder sister taught them nothing?

Chapter 16

A True Queen of England?

The account you have just read is the accepted story of the events that happened throughout Jane's life but in particular the events of 1553-1554. This is the story that has been passed down through history, the account that has been written in history books for years. Lady Jane Grey was manipulated and used by her father and the Duke of Northumberland and her mother was abusive and violent towards her, the very people in her life that were there to protect her. But is this account really true?

It is hard for us to look back and say with certainty one hundred percent one way or the other that it is because we simply were not there. We were not privy to every single conversation, present at every single meeting for every single minute of their lives. But as historians what we can do is look at the available evidence, the historical documents, the personal accounts of the people that were involved at the time and glean from them the truth. In the case of Jane's story have we fitted the details to suit our own narrative, or was something else going on here that history has forgotten? We certainly do not want to see Jane as a guilty party and no one can say she deserved her fate in any way but the events leading up to her death may not be as they seem. Henry Grey has been called many things but as a father, how could he allow this to happen to his daughter? Did Northumberland really have that level of power over the king and council and where did it all go wrong for him? Many historians have gone over the lead up to Edward's death and the events immediately afterward with a fine-tooth comb but are we just looking for someone to blame and he seemed the most likely person?

It is important to look at a potentional other outcomes to truly give a balanced and reasoned argument. One important point to remember is that most of what we know surrounding this time came through the foreign ambassadors for King Henri II of France and maybe more importantly through the Holy Roman Emperor Charles V but Ambassadors were not impartial, especially for Charles given his family ties to Mary, they would tell the facts as their master would want to know them and remember, they were not a neutral source!

Jane had entered the Tower of London as England's queen just seven months prior to her death and remains there 470 years later buried under the floor of the chapel of St Peter ad Vincula. Visitors to the Tower of London often seek out the final resting place of England's nine-day queen, she is a tragic heroine and her story has captured people's imaginations for centuries but we can only judge Jane and those around her by the standards of their day and not ours.

Life was very different in the mid-sixteenth century but the Tudors felt emotions just as we do, they loved and lost just as we do but it is always important to remember their morals were not the same as ours, making it difficult for us to pass judgement. Yes we can condemn Northumberland and Suffolk for their treatment of Jane and we are right to do so, but can we really understand the motives behind their actions given the scenario? Religion played no small part in the events of 1553/4 and to the power-hungry men of Tudor England the thought of a female ruler was beyond comprehension but when faced with no other alternative you would rather have a young, easily manipulated girl of your religious persuasion over a middle-aged catholic woman.

Crucially though Mary never based her claim to the throne on her religious notions. She claimed it was 'by act of parliament and the testament and last will of Henry VIII'. This is a very clever thing to do because by doing so she excludes no one. She accepted the help of any man willing to give it, regardless of their religious persuasion and we saw catholic and protestant alike flocking to her banner because they felt she was the rightful queen. Whereas Jane's supporters were reformists and made it clear from the start of their desires to rid the country of popery, the break from Rome would be final and lasting. When it came down to it, the people of England felt Mary's right was greater and religion did not become a factor, she was the eldest daughter of King Henry VIII and therefore the rightful queen of England.

So, let's go back to the beginning and look where Northumberland went wrong. King Edward VI is dying and the succession needs to be agreed, according to the last Will of his father, Henry VIII the next in line to succeed the throne is the Lady Mary, Henry's eldest child and daughter by Katherine of Aragon. She had been declared illegitimate but was nevertheless reinstated to the succession by her father in 1544 making it clear it was his intention for Mary to reign should Edward die childless. After Mary would come Elizabeth, daughter of Anne Boleyn and then so on and so on down the line, through the children and grandchildren of Henry's younger sister Mary.

The two Tudor half-sisters would remain illegitimate but could still claim the throne, Henry was more than likely assuming Edward would live a long life and have sons of his own so this scenario would never need to come up, but he put a plan in place just in case it did and it is just as well he did because Edward was to die young. There was never ever denying that Edward VI was true king of England, yes he was a minor but he still had the authority to overrule his ministers should he wish so why not have the right to name his own heir just like his father had? Henry made it so his heir could be announced by his Will, or by Letters Patent should he wish to make a last-minute change. It seems rather incongruous that one monarch can act in a certain way and then when another attempts the same thing his actions are questioned.

Edward wanted to amend the succession as was his right as monarch, he did not want his catholic sister Mary to inherit his crown and undo the religious works he had done but his first version of the Devise was not one that would see Northumberland gain any true power unless Jane gave birth to a son very early on in her marriage to Guildford. If she did then that little boy would be his grandson and he would have seen a Dudley sat on the throne of England in his own right. If Jane failed to conceive and give birth then Frances would assume to the role as protector of the realm until a legitimate baby boy was born. Frances does not come across as the kind of woman who could be easily manipulated, she definitely dominated her husband so from Northumberland's perspective, he stood little chance in ruling through her. So, was this the ammunition for Northumberland to force Edward to redraft the Devise to be more favourable to him? Quite possibly but there is no evidence to support that Northumberland forced Edward to change the Devise in favour of Jane. The most likely explanation for the re-write was the fact that Edward's illness was rapidly worsening and he knew he was dying and had no chance of having a child of his own and that there would be no time for Jane to conceive either.

The actions of Northumberland need to be looked at in more detail. If the Devise remained as it was to make it so the crown would pass to the first male born of the daughters of Frances Grey then there was a risk that Lady Katherine, who was also married at the same time as her sister could produce the all-important first male born child. Despite being much younger and it being unlikely her marriage would have been consummated straight away but there is no certainty Jane would have conceived and given birth to a son before her, she could have had three daughters like her mother. If Katherine gave birth to a boy first then she would have been regent for the young boy until he came of age and given her father-in-law was the Earl of Pembroke it seems unlikely Northumberland would have had the same kind of hold over her. So, the question is, did Northumberland 'advise' Edward to alter the devise so that it read Jane and her male born sons? The weddings took place in the May and the Devise was altered in the June; this is pretty compelling evidence of Northumberland possibly manipulating the king into altering the succession. But what of these marriages? What were the reasons behind them? One explanation could be that the marriages were planned prior to any plan made by Northumberland to seize the throne for Jane. Historian Eric Ives suggests in his book *Lady Jane Grey, A Tudor Mystery* that the idea of the marriages came via Lady Northampton and this is confirmed by William Cecil. On the face of it this could just have been two marriages between two prominent noble families of the time joining together as many did at the time. But if it was as simple as that why was Guildford chosen for Jane, she could have commanded a marriage to a first-born son of a duke so it seems an odd choice for Henry and Frances to agree to unless Northumberland was offering them more that a link to his family. There is no denying the marriage was certainly beneficial to Northumberland but could we not equally accuse Pembroke of trying to put Katherine on throne, arguably he did not have the same access to Edward to influence the succession but the thought must have crossed his mind and would explain the eagerness to have Katherine live with them straight after the marriage, whereas Jane returned home to her parents first.

At the time Edward wrote his Devise there were countless number of heirs to be chosen from, the problem for the king was they were all female and that was a situation he and his council had to accept. England was about to have its first Queen Regnant, the problem was in choosing who that should be. For whatever the reason was, Edward chose Jane and the wording was amended to include Jane **and** her male heirs. This put a whole new slant on the situation because it did not matter now if Jane conceived; she was next in line regardless. The addition of one word meant it became irrelevant as to whether or not a male heir existed for either sister. Northumberland would not have been keen for Jane to fall pregnant before she had claimed the throne because it could have brought an element of doubt to the councillors, was she carrying a male child, should they wait and see the outcome of the birth before claiming her the queen, it was better that Jane remained unpregnant. On the other hand, he needed the marriage to be consummated so she could not annul it once she became queen, the duke and duchess of Northumberland had to finely balance this marriage, Jane and Dudley were so young and naïve to the bigger picture, that his parents had to get it just right, by the time she was proclaimed queen they had certainly been living together at Durham House and would almost certainly shared a bed together.

There have been many accusations against Northumberland of using bribery to get the councillors to sign the Devise but is it realistic that he could have intimidated and coerced them all into signing a document that was so important to the country as a whole. We are talking about a group of powerful men, surely as a group they would have had the power to rise up against Northumberland and refuse to sign. Or had he convinced Edward so well that the councillors just did as their sovereign wished? Each member signed the declaration, Edward was their king and their loyalty to him clearly knew no bounds, in their eyes they were doing nothing more than obeying their monarch's wishes and that would be their defence when they later flocked to Mary's cause, turning their backs on Northumberland.

The question of whether the document was legally binding is an important one. Given that it had not been approved by Parliament would more than likely lend to the idea that it was not, all it does give us is a reflection of what Edward's supposed wishes were, regardless of whether Northumberland coerced him into it or not, Edward was a strong-minded young man, a king that demanded obedience from his subjects but he was in thrall to Northumberland and it may not have taken much persuasion to bend to his will, especially given his fragile health.

When Edward died Northumberland attempted to keep the news to himself to give him more time to move his pieces into position but he seems to dither too long, whilst he was stuttering news was travelling to Mary giving her the opportunity to gather her supporters to her cause. If Northumberland had been more proactive and attacked Mary earlier then the chances of his plan succeeding stood more chance of success. It appears he was unprepared, although considering he was in control of Edward he would have known death was close, so why the delay? Maybe he genuinely thought Mary would accept the news that Jane was to be queen although that seems unlikely too given the secrecy surrounding the Devise. Northumberland sent his son Robert to Hunsdon the morning after Edward had died only to find she had already left. Why not be more assertive and secure her person before Edward died, we could argue and say that no one knew exactly when he would die but if you were wanting to remove a threat then surely you would do that at the earliest possible opportunity. He could have had her put under house arrest at the very least at Hunsdon to keep her where he wanted.

One explanation for this is that he would not have wanted to alert people to his plans, it would have caused unrest amongst the people and risked too many questions being asked. In the end it seems Northumberland hesitated too much, underestimated Mary and missed his opportunity to seize the throne in Jane's name.

There were many delays and hesitations throughout Northumberland's plans. He delayed leaving London to try and track Mary down, it seems like he was apprehensive about taking her captive, he knew the Spanish would try and release her and by looking at the number of supporters she had, it was very unlikely they would just settle and accept Jane as their queen. If you add Spanish troops to the English supporters Northumberland would see the country over run and civil war would ensue.

Queen Mary got her throne but can we class Jane as a true queen of England? Yes, I think we can. She was proclaimed by the council, as every other monarch before her, on the 10 July 1553 in London and ruled for nine days. She may have been uncrowned but then so was Edward V, the tragic prince in the Tower and there is never any suggestion he was not the legitimate king at the time of his father's death. As a great-niece of Henry VIII, Jane was a legitimate claimant to the throne and is rightly listed on the website of our current Royal Family as being Queen of England.

Today Jane is seen as a tragic young girl who was used by men to gain their own advantage and there is no getting away from that fact. Yes, Jane was a headstrong and often at times rude young lady who had been utterly blindsided by her religion. She bordered on arrogance and insolence when it came to the topic of religion, she was right and if you were a catholic, then you were wrong and she was not willing to enter into a rational debate about that. Feckenham came closest to trying but he failed, she closed him down at every possible opportunity. Yet she was admired and praised for her theologian texts, giving her a reputation of being a wise and reasoned young woman. But the point of religion is often over-looked when we first think of Jane, the first image is of a young girl, blindfolded grasping at thin air in a panic as the block stands before her. A young innocent seventeen-year-old girl executed for being born into the royal house of Tudor. A young girl who faced her death with the upmost composure and bravery. A young girl who was abandoned by her family when she needed them most, her own parents left her to face her gruesome fate alone. I would like to think that Frances Grey shed a tear or two for her eldest child as her head was struck from her body. The daughter that had so much expectation on her young shoulders from birth that she was never going to be able to live up to. I hope Frances, and Henry whilst he was alive, felt some element of guilt for the role they played in their daughters downfall, or did they just see her as collateral damage? Jane had stood in the great hall at Syon house crying and pleading for her mother to help her, her mother reacted in a cold and callous manner telling her daughter it was Edward's wish that she take the crown. She then stood by and watched her child tremble with confusion and fear agree to take a crown she knew was not rightly hers. There are no records or evidence available to tell us how Frances coped with the death of her daughter but even the most hard hearted of mothers would grieve deeply over the loss of her child.

Appendix 1

Ordinances by Margaret, Countess of Richmond and Derby, as to what preparation is to be made against the deliverance of a Queen.

Taken from *Joannis Lelandi antiquarii De rebus Britannicis collectanea Third Volume, p279 onwards.*

Her Highnes Pleasure beinge understoode in what Chamber she will be delivered in, the same must be hanged with riche Clothe of Arras, Sydes, rowffe, Windowes and all, excepte one Windowe, which must be hanged so as she may have light when it pleasethe her. Then must there be set a Royall Bedde, and the Flore layed all over and over with Carpets, and a Cupboard covered with the same Suyte that the Chamber is hanged withall. Also there must be ordayned a faier Pallet, and all Things appertayninge therunto, and a riche Sparner hanginge over the same. And that Daye that the Queene (in good Tyme) will take her Chamber, the Chappell where her Highnes will receave and heare Devine Service, must be well and worshipfully arrayed. Also the greate Chamber must be hanged with riche Arras, with a Clothe and Chaire of Estate, and Quishins [cushions] thereto belonginge, the Place under and aboute the same beinge well encarped. Where the Queene (comminge from the Chappell with her Lords and Ladyes of Estate) may, either standinge or sittinge, at her Pleasure, receave spices and wyne. And the next Chamber betwixt the greate Chamber and the Queenes Chamber to be well and worshipfully hanged; which done, Two of the greatest Estats shall leade her to her Chamber, where they shall take their leave of her. Then all the Ladyes and Gentilwomen to goe in with her, and none to come unto the greate Chamber but Women; and Women to be made all Manner of Officers, as Butlers, Panters, sewers, & c. and all Manner of Officers shall bringe them all neadfull Thinges unto the greate Chamber Dore, and the Women Officers shall receave it there of them'.

Appendix 2

Act of the Six Articles 1539

Extract from Foxes Monuments, Ed Rev Geo Townsend (1846) Vol 5 p 262).

In this parliament, synod, or convocation, certain articles, matters, and questions, touching religion, were decreed by certain prelates, to the number especially of six, commonly called 'The Six Articles' (or, 'The Whip with Six Strings'), to be had and received among the king's subjects, on pretence of unity. But what unity thereof followed, the groaning hearts of a great number and also the cruel death of divers, both in the days of King Henry, and of Queen Mary, can so well declare as I pray God never the like be felt hereafter.

The doctrine of these wicked articles in the bloody Act contained, although it be worthy of no memory amongst Christian men, but rather deserveth to be buried in perpetual oblivion, yet, for that the office of history compelleth us thereunto, for the more light of posterity to come, faithfully and truly to comprise things done in the church, as well one as another, this shall be briefly to recapitulate the sum and effect of the aforesaid six articles, in order as they were given out, and hereunder do follow.

The first article in this present parliament accorded and agreed upon, was this That in the most blessed sacrament of the altar by the strength and efficacy of Christs mighty word (it being spoken by the priest), is present really, under the form of bread and wine, the natural body and blood of our Saviour Jesus Christ, conceived of the Virgin Mary; and that after the consecration there remaineth no substance of bread or wine, or any other substance, but the substance of Christ, God and man.

The Second Article.
That the communion in both kinds is not necessary 'ad salutern,' by the law or God, to all persons: and that it is to be believed, and not doubted of but that in the flesh, under form of bread, is the very blood, and with the blood, under form of wine, is the very flesh as well apart, as they were both together.

The Third Article.
That priests, after the order of priesthood received as before, may not marry by the law of God.

The Fourth Article.
That vows of chastity or widowhood, by man or woman made to God advisedly1 ought to be observed by the law of God; and that it exempteth them from other liberties of Christian people, which, without that, they might enjoy.

The Fifth Article.
That it is meet and necessary, that private masses be continued and admitted in this English church and congregation; as whereby good Christian people, ordering themselves accordingly, do receive both godly and goodly consolation. and benefits[2] and it is agreeable also to God's law.

The Sixth Article,
That auricular confession is expedient and necessary to be retained and continued, used and frequented, in the church of God.

1. Advisedly, that is made above the age of one and twenty years, priests only excepted.
2. By this, is meant, the helping of souls in purgatory.

The Act provided that all who denied the first should be burned as heretics. Those who persistently refused assent to the others should be hanged as felons. One immediate effect was that many zealous Reformers left the country and went to Germany and Switzerland where they joined with particularly the Zwinglian school.

In England it led to Latimer resigning the bishopric of Worcester and Shaxton that of Salisbury. It also compelled Cranmer to send his German (Lutheran) wife back to relatives and was only himself saved by the influence of the king. Although not enforced with relentless severity, the Act nevertheless resulted in over five hundred people being imprisoned.

Appendix 3

My deuise for the Succession 1553

1. For lakke of issu of my body To the L Franceses heires masles, if she have any such issu befor my death inserted to the L Janes and her heires masles, To the L Katerins heires masles, To the L Maries heires masles, To the heires masles of the daughters wich she shal haue hereafter. Then to the L Margets heires masles. For lakke of such issu, To theires masles of the L Janes daughters. To th'eires masles of the L Katerins daughters, and so forth til yow come to the L Margets heires masles.
2. If after my death theire masle be entred into 18 yere old, then he to have the hole rule and gouernauce therof.
3. But if he be under 18, then his mother to be gouuernres til he entre 18 yere old, But to doe nothing w'out th'auise and agremet of 6 parcel of a counsel to be pointed by my last will to the nombre of 20.
4. If the mother die befor th'eire entre into 18 the realme to be gouuerned by the cousel Prouided that after he be 14 yere al great matters of importaunce be opened to him.
5. If i died w'out issu, and there were none heire masle, then the L Fraunces to be (reget altered to) gouuernres. For lakke of her, the her eldest daughters,[4] and for lakke of them the L Marget to be gouuernres after as is aforsaid, til sume heire masle be borne, and then the mother of that child to be gouuernres.
6. And if during the rule of the gouuernres ther die 4 of the counsel, then shal she by her letters cal an assebe of the counsel w'in on month folowing and chose 4 more, wherin she shal haue thre uoices. But after her death the 16 shal chose emong themselfes til th'eire come to 14 yeare olde, and then he by ther aduice shal chose them

Appendix 4

Noted below is the full debate that took place between Lady Jane Grey and Dr John Feckenham entitled *'Perswasyons of Fecknam to turne the Lady Jane Dudley agaynst she shulde suffer deathe'* this was written in Jane's own hand and this transcript is taken from John Foxes *Acts and Monuments* (sometimes referred to as the *Book of Martyrs*) the debate between Jane and Feckenham was recorded and published by Foxe.

Feckenham: Madam, I lament your heavy case, and yet I doubt not, but that you bear out this sorrow of yours with a constant and patient mind.

Jane: You are welcome unto me, sir, if your coming be to give Christian exhortation. And as for my heavy case, I thank God, I do so little lament it, rather I account the same for a more manifest declaration of God's favour toward me, than he showed me at any time before. And therefore there is no cause why either you, or others which bear me good will, should lament or be grieved with this my case, being a thing so profitable for my soul's health.

Feckenham: I am here come to you at this present, sent from the queen and her council, to instruct you in the true doctrine of the right faith, although I have so great confidence in you, that I shall have, I trust, little need to travail with you much therein.

Jane: Forsooth, I heartily that the queen's Highness, which is not unmindful of her humble subject; and I hope, likewise, that you no

154

less will do your duty therein both truly and faithfully, according to that you were sent for.

Feckenham: What then is required of a Christian man?

Jane: That he should believe in God the Father, the Son, and the Holy Ghost, three persons, one God.

Feckenham: What? Is there nothing else to be required or looked for in a Christian, but to believe in him?

Jane: Yes, we must love him with all our heart, with all our soul, and with all our mind, and our neighbour as ourself.

Feckenham: Why? Then faith justifies not, or saves not.

Jane: Yes verily, faith, as Paul saith, only justifieth.

Feckenham: Why? St Paul saith, if I have all faith without love, it is nothing.

Jane: True it I; for how can I love him whom I trust not, or how can I trust him whom I love not? Faith and love go both together, and yet love is comprehended in faith.

Feckenham: How shall we love our neighbour?

Jane: To love our neighbour is to feed the hungry, to clothe the naked, and to give drink to the thirsty, and do to him as we would do to ourselves.

Feckenham: Why? Then it is necessary unto salvation to do good works also, and it is not sufficient only to believe.

Jane: I deny that, and I affirm that faith only saveth; but it is meet for a Christian, in token that he followeth his Master Christ, to do good works; yet may we not say that they profit from our salvation. For when we have done all, yet we be unprofitable servants, and faith only in Christ's blood saveth us.

Feckenham: How many sacraments are there?

Jane: Two - the one the sacrament of baptism and the other the sacrament of the Lord's supper.

Feckenham: No, there are seven.

Jane: By what Scripture find you that?

Feckenham: Well, we will talk of that hereafter. But what is signified by your two sacraments?

Jane: By the sacrament if baptism I am washed with water and regenerated by the Spirit, and that washing is a token to me that I am the child of God. The sacrament of the Lord's supper, offered unto me, is a sure seal and testimony that I am, by the blood of Christ, which he shed for me on the cross, made partaker of the everlasting kingdom.

Feckenham: Why? What do you receive in that sacrament? Do you not received the very body and blood of Christ?

Jane: No surely, I do not so believe. I think that at the supper I neither receive flesh nor blood, but bread and wine; which bread when it is broken, and the wine when it is drunken, put me in remembrance how that for my sins the body of Christ was broken, and his blood shed on the cross; and with that bread and wine I receive the benefits that come by the breaking of his body, and shedding of his blood, for our sins on the cross.

Feckenham: Why, doth not Christ speak these words, take eat, this is my body? Require you any plainer words? Doth he not say, it is his body?

Jane: I grant he saith so; and so he saith, I'm the vine, I am the door; but he is never more for that the door or the vine. Doth not St Paul say He calleth things that are not, as though they were? God forbid that I should say, that I eat the very natural body and blood of Christ; for then either I should pluck away my redemption, or else there were two bodies, or two Christs. One body was tormented on the cross, and if they did eat another body, then had two bodies; or if his body were eaten, then was it not broken upon the cross; or if it were broken upon the cross, it was not eaten of his disciples.

Feckenham: Why, is it not as possible that Christ, by his power, could make his body both the be eaten and broken, and to be born of a virgin, as to walk upon the sea, having a body, and other suchlike miracles as he wrought by his power only?

Jane: Yes verily, if God would have done at his supper and miracle, he might have done so; but I say, that then he minded no work nor miracle but only to break his body and shed his blood on the cross for our sins. But I pray you to answer me to this one question; Where was Christ when he said, Take, eat, this is my body? Was he not at the table, when he said so? he was at the time alive, and suffered not till the next day. What took he, but bread? What brake he, but bread? And what gave he, but bread? Look, what he took, he brake; and look, what he brake, he gave; and look, what he gave, they did eat; and yet all this while he himself was alive, and at supper before his disciples, or else they were deceived.

Feckenham: Your ground your faith upon such authors as say and unsay both in a breath; and not upon the church, to whom ye ought to give credit.

Jane: No, I ground My faith on God's word, and not upon the church. For if the church be a good church, the faith of the church must be tried by God's word; and not God's word by the church, neither yet my faith. Shall I believe the church because of antiquity, or shall I give credit to the church that taketh away from me the half part of the Lord's Supper, and will not let man receive it in both kinds? Which things, if they deny to us, then deny they to us part of our salvation. And I say, that it is an evil church, and not the spouse of Christ, but the spouse of the devil, that altereth the Lord's supper, and both taketh from it, and addeth to it. To that church say I, God will add plagues; and from that church will he take their part out of the book of life. Do they learn that of St Paul, when he ministered to the Corinthians in both kinds? Shall I believe this church? God forbid!

Feckenham: That was done for a good intent of the church, to avoid a heresy that sprang on it.

Jane: Why, shall the church alter God's will and ordinance, for good intent? How did King Saul? The Lord God defend!

After this Feckenham took his leave, saying he was sorry for me, for I am sure, quoth he, that we two shall never meet. True it is, said I, that we shall never meet, except God turn your heart; for I am assured, unless you repent and turn to God, you are in an evil case; and I pray God, in the bowels of his mercy, to send you his Holy Spirit; for he hath given you his great gift of utterance; if it pleased him also to open the eyes of your heart.

Appendix 5

Below is the letter Jane wrote to her sister Katherine from the Tower of London before her execution in February 1554. It has been taken from *Acts and Monuments Volume VI* by John Foxe.

I Haue here sente you (good sister Katherin) a booke, which although it bee not outwardlye trimmed with golde, yet inwardly it is more worth then precious stones: it is the boke (dere Sister) of the lawe of the Lorde. It is his testament and last wil, which he bequethed vnto vs wretches, which shall lead you to the pathe of eternall ioye: and if you with a good mind read it, and with an earnest minde do folow it, it shal bring you to an immortall and euerlasting life. It wil teache you to liue, and learne you to die. It shal winne you more then you shoulde haue gained by the possession of your wofull fathers lāds. for, as if god had prospered him you shuld haue inherited his lāds: so if you apply diligētly this boke, sekyng to directe your life after it, you shalbe an inheritor of such riches, as nether the couetous shal withdraw from you, neither thefe shal steale, nether yet the mothes corrupt. Desyre with Dauid (good sister) tunderstād the law of the lord your god: liue stil to die, that you (by death) may purchase eternal lyfe. And truste not that the tenderousnes of your age shal lēghthen your life. For as soone (if God call) goeth the yong as the olde: & labour alwayes to learn to die, de e the worlde, denye the deuill, and despise the eshe, and delite your selfe onely in the Lord. Be penitent for your sinnes, and yet despaire not: be strong in faith, & yet presume not, and desire with saint Paule to be dissolued, and to be with Christ, with whom euē in death ther is life. Be like the good seruaunt, & euen at mid night be waking, lest when death commeth and stealeth vpon you like a thefe in the nighte, you be with the euyll seruaunt found sleping, & lefte for lacke of oyle, you be founde like the ue foolish women, and lyke hym that had not on the weddyng garment, and then ye be cast out from the mariage. Reioyce in Christ, as I trust I do. Folow the steppes of your maister Christ, and take vp your crosse, lay your sinnes on his back and alwaies embrace him. And as touching my death, reioyce as I doe (good Sister) that I shal be deliuered of this corruption, and put on incorruption. For I am assured that I shall for losyng of a mortall lyfe, wynne an immortal lyfe, the whiche I praye God graunt you, sende you of his grace to liue in his feare, and to die in the true christian fayth, from the whiche (in Gods name) I exhort you that you neuer swarue, neither for hope of life, nor for feare of death. For if ye wyl deny his truth to lenghthen youre lyfe, God wyll denye you, and yet shorten youre dayes. And if you will cleaue vnto him, he will prolong your dayes to your comforte and hys glory, to the whiche glory god bring me nowe, and you hereafter when it pleaseth hym to call you. Fare you well (good Sister) and put your onely trust in god, who onely muste helpe you.

Appendix 6

Proclamation of Lady Jane Grey as Queen of England, 1553

Taken from *Londini in ædibus Richardi Graftoni Reginæ & in excusum Anno Domini M.D.LIII Cum priuilegio ad imprimen-dum solum*

Iane by the grace of God Quene of England, Fraunce And Ireland, defendor of the faith, & of the Church of Englande, & Also of Irelande vnder Christ in earth the supreme head. To al our most louing, faithfull, and obedient subiects, and to euery of them greting. Where our moste dere cousin Edwarde the vi. late King of England, Fraunce and Ireland, defendour of the faith, and in Earth the supreme head vnder Christ of the Church of Englande And Irelande, by his letters patentes signed with his owne hand, And sealed with his great seale of Englande, bearing date of xxi. day of June, in the vii. yere of his reigne, in the presence of the most parte of his nobles, his counsailours, Judges, and diuerse others graue, and sage personages for the profite and suretie of the whole realme therto assenting, and subscribing their names to the same, hath by the same his Lettres Patentes recited, that forasmuch as the Imperiall croune of this realme, by an Acte made in the xxxv. yere of the reigne of the late King of woorthy memory King Henrie the viii. our progenitour, and great uncle, was for lacke of issue of his bodie lawfullie begotten, and for lacke of issue of the bodie of our saide late cosin King Edwarde the vi. by the same act limited, and appointed to remaine to the Ladie Marie, by the name of the ladie Marie his eldest Daughter, and to the Heires of her bodie lawfully begotten, and for default of such

161

issue, the remainder therof to the Ladie Elizabeth, by the name of the Ladie Elizabeth his seconde Daughter, and to the heires of her bodie lawefully begotten, with such condicions, as shoulde be limited, and appointed by the saied late King of woorthie memorie, King Henrie theight our progenitour, and great vncle by his letters patentes vnder his great Seale, or by his last wil in writing signed with his hande. And forasmuch as the saied limitation of Thimperial croune of this realme, being limited (as is aforesaid) to the said Ladie Marie, and Ladie Elizabeth being illegitimate, and not lawfully begotten, for that that the mariage had betweene the saied late King, King Henrie theight our progenitour, and great vncle, and the Ladie Katherine mother to the saied Ladie Marie, & also the mariage had betwene the saied late king, King Henrie theight our progenitor and great vncle, and the ladie Anne mother to the saied ladie Elizabeth, were cleerely, and lawfully vndone by sentences of deuorces, according to the woorde of God, and the Ecclesiasticall lawes: And which saied seueral deuorcements have beene seuerally ratified, & confirmed by auctoritie of parlament, and especiallie in the xxviii.yere of the reigne of King Henrie theight our said progenitor, and great vncle, remaining in force, strength, and effect, wherby aswel the said Ladie Marie, as also the said Ladie Elizabeth, to all ententes, and purposes, are, and been cleerely disabled, to aske, claime, or chalenge the saied Imperiall croune, or any other of the honours, castelles, manours, Lordshippes, lands, tenements, or other hereditaments, as heire, or heires to our said late cosin King Edward the vi.or as heire, or heires to any other person, or persons whosoeuer, aswel for the cause before rehearsed, as also for that that the saied Lady Marie, and Lady Elizabeth were vnto our saied late cosin but of the halfe bloud, and therefore by the ancient lawes. statutes, and customes of this realme be not inheritable vnto our saied late Cosin, although they had beene borne in lawefull Matrimonie, as in dede they were not, as by the saied sentences of deuorce, and the saied statute of the xxviii.yere of the reigne of King Henrie the eight our saied progenitor and great Uncle, plainly appeareth.

And forasmuch also as it is to be thought, or at the least, much to be doubted, that if the saied ladie Marie, or ladie Elizabeth should hereafter haue, & enjoy the said Imperial croune of this realm and should then happen to marry with any Stranger borne out of this realme, that then the same Stranger hauing the gouernmente and the Imperiall Crowne in his handes, would adhere and practise, not onely to bring this noble free realme, into the tirannie and seruitude of the Bishoppe of Rome, but also to haue the lawes and customes of his or their own natiue countrey or countreys to be practised, and put in vre within this realme, rather then the laws, statutes, and customes here of long time vsed, wherupon the title of inheritance of all and singular the subiects of this realme dooe depend, to the peril of conscience, and the vtter subuersion of the common weale of this realme wherupon our saied late dere cosin weighing and considering with himselfe, what waies and meanes were most conuenient to be had for the stay of the said succession in the saied Imperiall croune, if it should please God to call our said late cosin out of this transitory life, hauing no issue of his body, and calling to his remembrance that wee and the Lady Katherine, and the Lady Mary our sisters, being the daughters of the lady Fraunces our natuerall mother, and then and yet wife to our naturall & most louing father Henrie Duke of Suffolke, and the lady Margaret: daughter of the lady Elianour then deceassed sister of the said lady Fraunces, and the late wife of our cosin Henrie Erle of Comberland, were very nigh of his graces bloud, of the part of his fathers side our said progenitour and great vncle, and being naturally borne here within the realme, and for the very good opinion our said late cosin had of our, and our said sisters and cosin Margarets good education, did therefore vpon good deliberation and aduise heerin had and taken, by his said Letters Patents declare, ordre, assigne, limit, and appoinct, that if it should fortune himselfe our said late cosin king Edward the sixt to decease, hauing no issue of his body lawfully begotten, that then the saied Imperiall croune of England and Ireland, and the confines of the same, and his title to the croune of the realme of France, and all and singular honors, castles, prerogatiues, priuiledges, preheminences, aucthorities, iurisdictions, dominions, possessions, and hereditaments, to our said late cosin King Edward the sixt, or to the said Imperiall croune belonging, or in any wise appertaining, should for lacke of such issue of his body remain, come, and be unto the eldest sonne of the body of the said lady Fraunces lawfully begotten, being borne into the world in his life time, and to the heires males of the body of the same eldest sonne lawfully begotten, and so from sonne to sonne as he should be of auncienty in birth, of the body of the said lady Fraunces lawfully begotten, being borne into the world in our said late cosins life time, and to the heires males of the boy of euery such sonne lawfully begotten:and for default of such sonne borne into the world in his life time, of the body of the said lady Fraunces lawfully begotten, and for lack of heires males of euery such sonne lawfully begotten, that then the sayd Imperial croune, and all & singular other the premisses should remain, come, and be to us, by the name of lady Jane, eldest daughter of the said lady Fraunces, & to the heires males of our body lawfully begotten, and for lacke of such heire male of our body lawfully begotten, that then the sayd Imperial croune, and all other the premisses should remain, come, & be to the sayd lady Katherine our sayd second sister, and the heires males of the boy of the sayd lady Katherine lawfully begotten, with diuerse other remainders, as by the same letters patents more plainly & at large it may and doeth appere. Sithens the making of which letters patents, that is to say on Thursday, which was the vi. day of this instant moneth of July, it hath pleased God to cal to his infinite mercy our sayd most dere & entirely beloued cosin Edard the vi. whose soule God pardon, & forasmuch as he is now deceased, hauing no heires of his body begotten, & that also there remaineth at this present time no heires lawfully begotten of the body of our sayd progenitor, and great vncle king Henrie theight, and forasmuch also as the sayd lady Fraunces our sayd mother, had no issue male begotten of her body, and borne into the worlde, in the life time of our saied cosin King Edward the sixth, so as the saied Imperiall croune, and other the premisses

164

to the same belonging, or in any wise appertayning, now be, and remaine to vs in our actuall, and royall possession by auctority of the sayd letters patents: wee doe therefore by these presents signifie vnto all our most louing, faithfull, and obedient subiects, that like as we for our part shall, by Goddes grace, shew our selfe a most gracious, and benigne Souuereine Queene, and Lady to all our good Subiects in all their iust, and lawfull sutes, and causes, and to the vttermost of our power shal preserue and maintaine Gods most holy word, christian policy, and the good laws, customes, and liberties of these our realmes & dominions: So we mistrust not, but they, and euery of them wil again see their partes, at all times, and in all cases shew themselues vnto vs their naturall liege Queene, and Lady, most faythfull, louing, and obedient subiects, according to their bounden duties, and allegeaunces, whereby they shall please God, and doe the thing that shall tend to their own preseruations, and sureties: Willing, and commanding all men of all estates, degrees, and condicions, to see our peace, and accord kept, and to bee obedient to our Lawes, as they tender our fauor, and will answere for the contrary, at their exreme perils. In witnes whereof, wee haue caused these our letters to bee made patents. Witnesse our selfe at our Towre of London, the tenth day of Julie, in the first yeere of our reigne.

God save the Queene.

Bibliography

Primary Sources

Haynes, S. *A Collection of State Papers, Relating to Affairs in the Reigns of King Henry VIII. King Edward VI. Queen Mary, and Queen Elizabeth*, (William Bowyer, London 1740)

Secondary Sources

Borman, T. *Elizabeth's Women: The Hidden Story of the Virgin Queen*, (Vintage, London, 2010)

Borman, T. *The Private Lives of the Tudors: Uncovering the secrets of Britain's Greatest Dynasty*, (Hodder & Stoughton, London, 2016)

Byrne, C. *Lady Katherine Grey: A Dynastic Tragedy*, (The History Press, Cheltenham, 2023)

Cook, F. *Lady Jane Grey, Nine Day Queen of England*, (Evangelical Press, Leyland, 2004)

Davy, R. *The sisters of Lady Jane Grey and their Wicked Grandfather; being the true stories of the strange lives of Charles Brandon, Duke of Suffolk, and of the ladies Katherine and Mary Grey, sisters of Lady Jane Grey, "the nine-days' queen*, (E.P. Dutton & Co, New York, 1912)

De Lisle, L. *The Sisters who would be Queen*, (Harper Press, London, 2008)

De Lisle, L. *Tudor: The Family Story* (Chatto and Windus, London, 2013)

Guy, J. *Tudor England*, (Oxford University Press, Oxford, 1988)

Guy, J. *Elizabeth: The Forgotten Years*, (Viking, London, 2016)

Hilton, L. *Elizabeth: Renaissance Prince, A Biography*, (Weidenfeld & Nicholson, London, 2015)

Ives, E. *Lady Jane Grey: A Tudor Mystery*, (Wiley-Blackwell, Chichester, 2011)

Lelandi, J. *Antiquarii De rebus Britannicis Collectanea Third Volume, p279 onwards.* Accessed via Google Books on 21 July 2023.

Licence, Amy. *Tudor Roses: From Margaret Beaufort to Elizabeth I,* (Amberley Publishing, Stoud, 2022)

Lipscomb, S. *The King is Dead: The Last Will and Testament of Henry VIII*, (Head of Zeus, London 2015)

Paul, J. *The House of Dudley: A New History of Tudor England*, (Michael Joseph, London, 2022)

Plowden, A. *Lady Jane Grey: Nine Days Queen*, (The History Press, Stroud, 2016)

Porter, L. *Mary Tudor: The First Queen*, (Piatkus Books, London, 2009)

Tallis, N. *Crown of Blood: The Deadly Inheritance of Lady Jane Grey*, (Michael O'Mara Books Limited, London, 2017)

Tallis, N. Elizabeth's Rival: *The Tumultuous Life of Lettice Knollys, Countess of Leicester*, (Michael O'Mara Limited, London, 2018)

Weir, A. *The Six Wives of Henry VIII,* (The Bodley Head, London, 1991)

Weir, A. *Children of England: The Heirs of King Henry VIII* 1547-1558. (Johnathan Cape, London, 2015)

Weir, A. *Henry VIII: King and Court*. (Vintage, London, 2020)

Whitelock, A. *Mary Tudor: England's First Queen*. (Bloomsbury Publishing, London. 2010)

Whitelock, A. *Elizabeth's Bedfellows: An Intimate History of the Queen's Court,* (Bloomsbury, London, 2013)

Wooding, L. *Tudor England: A History*, (Yale University Press, London, 2022)

Internet Sources

Joannis Lelandi Antiquarii de rebus britannicis collectanea - John Leland - Google Books

https://archive.org/details/actsmonumentsofj05foxeuoft/page/262

www.sudeleycastle.co.uk

https://www.nationalarchives.gov.uk/

Spain: July 1553, 1-10 | British History Online (british-history.ac.uk)

Index

Mary, Queen of Scots, 55, 60, 72

Mary Tudor, Queen of France and later Duchess of Suffolk, 2-5, 13

Morgan, Sir Richard, 117

Offley, Thomas, 130

Paget, William, 61, 105

Parr, Katherine, Dowager Queen of England, 42, 44-6, 48-50

Parr, William, Marquess of Northampton, 10, 60, 112-13

Partridge, Nathaniel, 106

Paulet, William, Marquess of Winchester, 94

Pole, Cardinal Reginald, 107, 121

Renard, Simon, 123

Ridley, Nicholas, 101

Scheyfve, Jean 80, 92, 111

Seymour, Edward, Duke of Somerset and Lord Protector, 37-8, 42, 50, 61-3, 70, 138

Seymour, Edward, Earl of Hertford, 58-138

Seymour, Jane, Queen of England, 19, 22

Seymour, Margery, 49

Seymour, Thomas, Baron Seymour of Sudeley, 37, 40, 42-4, 47-8, 50, 52, 55-61

Sharington, Sir William, 55

Stewart, Matthew, Earl of Lennox, 35

Stuart, Henry, Lord Darnley, 36

Stokes, Adrian, 136

Tilney, Elizabeth, 130, 133

Tudor, Margaret, Queen of Scotland, 8, 34, 75

Weston, Hugh, 135

Wharton, Lady Anne, 64

Willoughby, Catherine, Duchess of Suffolk, 7, 15, 69

Wolsey, Cardinal Thomas, 2, 5

Wotton, Margaret, 9, 11, 14, 17, 24

Wyatt, Sir Thomas, 122, 124-5